Fundamentals of Contract and Commercial Management

IACCM

International Association for
Contract & Commercial Management

Colophon

Title:	Fundamentals of Contract and Commercial Management
	Based on original concepts by IACCM
IACCM Project Director:	Bob Emery
Reviewers:	Judy Ballou
	Tim Cummins
	Mark David
	Bob Emery
	Adrian Furner
	Diane Homolak
	Timothy S McCarthy
	Nancy J Nelson
	Gianmaria Riccardi
	Jason Waterman
Copy Editor:	Jane Chittenden
Publisher:	Van Haren Publishing, Zaltbommel, www.vanharen.net
ISBN Hard copy:	978 90 8753 712 8
ISBN eBook:	978 90 8753 713 5
Print:	First edition, first impression, October 2013

Contents

Acknowledgments

IACCM wishes to thank the international team of experts who contributed and reviewed the manuscript. The reviewers and contributors have diligently and professionally spent much time in making sure that expertise gained over many years is conveyed throughout this book. More than that, an immense amount of time and thought has been made to ensure that what can sometimes seem a complex topic is explained in an engaging and thought-provoking manner.

This project was made particularly special by the many contributors and supporters of IACCM whose humor and support drove the professional delivery of the manuscript. Rarely has a project been delivered with such strong team camaraderie and mutual support.

Team

Judy Ballou	Retired
Tim Cummins	CEO, IACCM
Mark David	Author and Consultant
Adrian Furner	Director & Founding Partner, Kommercialize Limited
Diane Homolak	Legal Operations Quality and Strategy Manager, HP
Timothy S McCarthy	Director, Contracting and Negotiations, Rockwell Automation
Nancy J Nelson	Director, Contracts and Commercial Management (Shared Services) CSC
Gianmaria Riccardi	Global Commercial Director, Cisco Systems
Jason Waterman	Senior Procurement Advisor, UK Cabinet Office

Foreword

Study the headlines from around the world and you will rapidly grasp the significance of contract management. Stories abound of multi-billion losses in whatever currency you choose to name—$30bn from weaknesses in US defense contracts, €140bn from failed European software projects, £300 million each year on UK Government service contracts. Cancelled projects, failed development initiatives, even losses of human life are increasingly attributed to poor contracts.

However, the real failing is not the contract, but rather it is poor contracting practices. It is people who decide on the form, structure or terms of a contract and the way it will be managed. As business people we all have a role in ensuring that contracts are designed, developed, negotiated and managed in a way that is 'fit for purpose'.

Today's trading relationships are in many ways more complex than those of the past. Factors such as globalization, increased regulation, innovative technologies, and the speed of change have all contributed to an environment in which it is often difficult to define and manage the many factors involved in a successful contract. This has led many organizations to see the contract primarily as an instrument of control, where rigid standards are imposed and negotiation is restricted to specialists. Unfortunately, this thinking has led to many business people stepping away from their role in the process, viewing the contract as a purely legal or procedural requirement. The consequences of this are reflected in the headline losses mentioned above.

This book seeks to provide insight to the good contracting practices that will contribute to business success. As a simple introductory example, let's look briefly at the way that today's sales and purchasing practices have contributed to poor contracts and resulted in avoidable losses.

Procurement organizations have been tasked with saving money. They perceive suppliers trying to undermine these efforts through specific techniques:

- Forming relationships with the business people and thereby working around Procurement.
- Exaggerating product or service performance to justify a higher price.
- 'Bundling' products or services into 'solutions' that make competitive price comparisons difficult.
- Offering a low initial contract price, but with contracting practices that mask incremental charges or expensive change procedures.

Procurement has developed a variety of methods to protect against these techniques:

- Controlling or forbidding direct conversation with the business people
- Onerous performance penalties in the form of damages, service level credits and other 'penalties'
- An approach known as 'commoditization', which seeks to unbundle a supplier's offering to allow direct competitive comparison.
- Growing insistence on the use of their own standard terms and conditions, leading to a low-value 'battle of the forms'.
- A more adversarial approach in post-award performance management to restrict price or charge increases and overruns.

The combination of these techniques and methods has a negative impact on contract formation and the results achieved. This can be avoided only through patiently forming a positive, multi-tiered relationship that includes developing the right contract structure and terms. A supplier must help its customers appreciate that constraints on conversation, imposition of ill-suited standard contracts or the unbundling of genuine added-value solutions is detrimental to their own interests, but this can be done only by tackling these issues at the right levels, with the right experts and at the right time.

Introduction

Why do I need to know anything about contracts?

That's a question many people ask and which this book will answer. Contracts are fundamental to a business and its value. Just think for a moment how much you would be willing to pay for a business that had no contracts? Or why it is that investors flee from companies that show themselves unable to manage or enforce their contracts?

Most adults have managed a contract without even realizing it. Take the example of a man looking out of the front window of his house on a snowy day. He sees a young man walking by with a snow shovel. The young man sees him in the window and raises his shovel with a quizzical look on his face. The older man reaches into his pocket and pulls out his hand with money in it. The young man holds up ten fingers. The older man nods, steps away from the window, and the young man shovels the walk. After the young man finishes the walk and rings the bell, the older man opens the door, surveys the walk, and pays him ten dollars.

Expending minimal effort and time, these two men have completed a business transaction and actually managed a very simple contract from initiation to completion without the use of a single word or piece of paper. Business transactions demand more formal communication and record-keeping, but most commerce in our world follows that same process. Understanding the process and how to facilitate its important elements is fundamental to driving business objectives and success.

Making and managing contracts can be hard work, or it can be easy. A goal of this book is to combine commercial process knowledge with an understanding of the roles in the buyer/seller relationship to make contracting both efficient and effective.

Even the simple example of the snow shoveler highlights the fundamental questions that all business people have about any transaction:

- Is it clear what is wanted, and when?
- Will it be at an acceptable price?
- Can what is promised be delivered?

As the situation becomes more complex, so do the questions we ask:

- Is what is promised what the customer thinks they're going to get?
- Does the contract offer an acceptable return?
- Does the contract make the best use of available resources?
- Do I understand the risks involved and my part in managing them?
- When things change, what happens?
- If it all goes horribly wrong, what are the consequences?

Most business people ask these basic questions routinely. Asking, answering, and documenting these questions is the most fundamental level of contract and commercial management, and it is this that makes almost everyone a contract manager, whether consciously or unconsciously.

Beyond this statement is the professional reality that contract or commercial management is often one of the least defined positions in the corporate hierarchy. Consequently, individuals with many different titles perform some or all of the elements of the process we will talk about within this book as the commercial transaction process. Whether the reader's job title is Managing Director or Accounting Clerk, that position touches the transaction process, and understanding the value added by the contract manager enables each to function more effectively. It also means we have a collective responsibility to make the contracts in our organization contribute to its success rather than become a source of poor performance and loss.

Readers can work through each chapter of this book in sequence or select individual chapters of interest that relate to a specific job function. This is not designed to be an operational guide or give detailed instructions in the duties of contract management. Its purpose

is to provide a broad commercial audience with an overview of the fundamental functions of contract management, the unique perspective and skills that dedicated professionals can bring to the transaction process. It is also designed to challenge the reader to facilitate business through understanding the process and improving its function as individual abilities and situations permit.

Part One: Essentials provides a general overview of the transaction process and the types of relationships encountered; the main elements of a contract; cost, pricing and payment; and negotiation principles. This Part concludes with an overview of the commercial transaction process. These early chapters contain checklists and questions the reader can use to identify key issues.

Part Two: The contract management lifecycle takes the reader through each of the five phases of the lifecycle, starting with initiation of a project, bidding, developing and negotiating a contract. The remaining chapters in this Part address the Manage phase: contract implementation, managing day-to-day performance and issues that must be addressed to move the project forward to a successful completion rather than a costly dispute. Questions and checklists have again been provided to aid in issue identification.

Case studies are included throughout the text to demonstrate the real-world application of the issues. Appendices are included that contain relevant supplementary information.

Each step of the commercial transaction process is covered, including a description of the step and the critical duties that must be performed. Perhaps more important is a discussion of the reason why the step is important to the business and the value that a professional can add to the process.

This book will enable readers to approach this process with greater knowledge, confidence and understanding, providing them with the edge to improve performance.

PART 1
ESSENTIALS

CHAPTER 1
COMMERCIAL RELATIONSHIPS: BUILDING A FOUNDATION

Business is not just doing deals; business is having great products, doing great engineering, and providing tremendous service to customers. Finally, business is a cobweb of human relationships.

Ross Perot

1.1 *The relationship continuum*

The business world is full of relationships, with the most pervasive or critical being the one between buyer and seller. Every individual, regardless of title or other duties, is at some point involved with or affected by these relationships. Career and business success or failure can often be attributed to these interactions

Business relationships reside in a complex universe with infinite variables. While many have tried to document these, there is no global standard that applies across industries, geographies and types of product or service. One way to express this is as a continuum in terms of relative depth and complexity (Figure 1.1).

At the far left side of the continuum is the purchase or sale of a commodity item, which is generally executed with a simple transaction that may be repetitive. At the far right side of the continuum is the purchase or sale of products, systems, or services that are critical to business performance. These sales are generally the result of a relationship that is built and developed through several transactions between the buyer and seller.

Business efficiency demands that the right amounts of effort and resources are invested in each transaction. Understanding the big

Figure 1.1   The relationship continuum

picture and where we fall on the continuum as both buyers and sellers enables us to properly focus our energies.

The relationships can also be seen as a pyramid, where there are numerous relationships at the lower levels and few at the top (Figure 1.2).

To provide an illustration of the different buyer/seller relationships, let's look at a common item such as office supplies. At the first level we could consider a supplier of common items such as light bulbs, pens and paper. While variety and cost may be extensive, we are basically looking at a commodity where comparisons of value are easy to make. Commodities are generally considered to be consumable and are not usually capital expenditures.

Moving beyond a strict commodity we go to a category where some corporate standards are imposed. These purchases are usually of a higher value or considered capital expenditures. There will potentially be questions around functionality and fit. Following the office supplies

Figure 1.2   Customer relationship levels

example, this might be the standard office equipment of desk and chair, filing cabinets, floor coverings etc. Any supplier meeting the standards could provide the item.

Transactions and suppliers move from this category of functional to value-added through exceptional performance or through additional services that are harder to copy or replicate. In the previous example, a supplier of the basic functional furnishings may move to this tier by offering free delivery, assembly, or design services, or through providing customized upholstery including corporate logos.

The final step of the continuum is that of consultant/critical business advisor. This relationship stands apart because of its role in the success of the business or some aspect of it. This supplier is often in a position to prevent or resolve other business problems through its understanding of the customer's operations and creatively positioning its services and solutions to meet those needs. Continuing with the original example, this could be a designer or marketing professional who helped develop a corporate identity and translated that through to office designs, particularly in corporate space, or it might be an outsourced provider who takes full responsibility for minimizing cost and maximizing productivity through a customized office supplies service.

Suppliers of a commodity: In this relationship a supplier's product is viewed by the customer as being exactly the same as several (or perhaps many) other products that meet the same specifications, grade and quality. Price and availability are the traditional differentiating factors in trading of commodities. Other examples might be paper goods, heating oil, hardware or any other product where there is little differentiation and no services are provided.

Suppliers of functioning equipment/systems: The seller is seen as a supplier of functioning equipment or systems with quality and reliability and a service that meets the customer's minimum standards. Examples might include suppliers of computer servers, large-scale copiers, or corporate vehicles.

Value-added products/systems and service: The seller is viewed as a reliable and value-added supplier of products and services. Contractual

arrangements are fulfilled on time, products are provided conveniently, and additional services may be provided such as training, technical or financing support. At this level, price remains important, but may not be the main criterion. The customer becomes less likely to shop around with competitors and the cost of switching may be high. Suppliers who are unwilling or unable to provide the extras cease to be competitors. Examples might include suppliers of integrated technology, engineering or construction services.

Consultant/critical business advisor: This relationship is based on not only providing value-added products and systems and extra service, but on helping the customer to deal better with some of its important business issues. The seller's contribution is made by understanding the customer's business situation and objectives, by generating workable ideas for solving problems, taking advantage of opportunities, jointly planning with the customer, being sensitive to the customer's organizational issues, and being viewed by the customer as a business partner. Examples include large outsourcing relationships, especially in an area such as business process outsourcing, or high-value strategic consulting.

Looking across the continuum it is easy to see that the relationship within each category is different. On the transaction side, the costs and risks associated with switching suppliers are minimal and customer loyalty is generally low. Moving across the continuum those costs and risks increase exponentially along with the investment by both buyers and sellers.

We can see how these relationships are changing over time, with emerging needs for business success (Figure 1.3).

A business relationship may begin with a transaction buyer purchasing a commodity and progresses through time to a relationship buyer purchasing strategic supplies and solutions. A supplier may foster this relationship evolution by offering volume purchasing incentives or partnering with other vendors to provide enhanced solutions. When a buyer recognizes the additional benefits and business value that can be achieved, it assists this transition by discussing its overall needs with suppliers so that they can better respond to an increased requirement.

Emerging Needs for Success

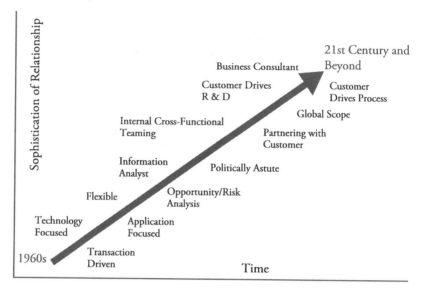

Figure 1.3   How business relationships are changing

The transaction buyer: This customer can easily switch all parts of its purchasing from one supplier to another. There are low internal costs of switching between suppliers. This makes it easy for a new supplier to penetrate the customer base and harder for an incumbent to defend. Price, features, support, and delivery intervals are important decision criteria. Timeframes between purchasing decisions are usually short. For the buyer, making comparisons between suppliers is easy and they can maximize their negotiating power; for this reason, many buyers try to 'commoditize' every purchase.

The relationship buyer: This customer faces high costs of switching suppliers and changes suppliers reluctantly, because changes require substantial investment. Due to the critical nature of the product and/or service to the customer's business, the perceived risk of changing is high. The customer is concerned about issues such as the supplier's focus on research and development (R&D), product continuity and future business health. This customer base is difficult for the outsider to penetrate, but easier for the incumbent to defend. It also changes the

relative power of the supplier and customer during negotiation and performance.

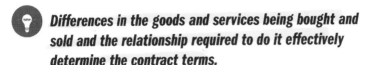

> **Differences in the goods and services being bought and sold and the relationship required to do it effectively determine the contract terms.**

1.2 Using contracts to document commercial relationships

Modern commercial enterprises operate in a world of rapid change. Expectations are rising, pressures to reduce costs are escalating, and high standards of quality and service are now entry-level requirements for a supplier of goods and services. Many different types of commercial relationship are formed to serve these needs, and that means different contracts are required. Some frequently used types of relationships or agreements requiring contractual arrangements include:

- Teaming and partnering agreements
- Franchises, distribution agreements
- Agency and representative agreements
- License and right to use agreements
- General sales agreements
- Service agreements
- Outsourcing agreements
- Engineer, build and install agreements
- Professional consulting agreements
- Standard purchase orders

All of these types of business arrangements require specific understanding of the roles and responsibilities and the expectations from each party. There are some who argue that today's fast moving business environment has reduced the importance of the contract. They say, "It's the relationship that matters". In reality, the extent of change and the need for speed actually increase the importance of a foundational agreement that accurately records the underlying business objectives and associated commitments. This understanding of the rights and obligations of both parties provides a framework for the management of change, whether due to altered business conditions, new technologies, evolving requirements or regulations, or resulting from a merger or acquisition.

 Benefits of effective contract management

Improved quality of service and customer focus

Greater value for money and cost control

Reduced crisis management

Decreased level of risk

Effective implementation in relation to changes or development in the market

Continued improvement through incentive based contracting and risk sharing

Early identification and resolution of poor contract performance and associated problems and disputes

Controls over performance, costs and standards

Identification of things that worked well and not so well to inform and benefit future contracts

Few businesses stay the same. Contracts and relationships must evolve along with the business to reflect the current environment and risks. They should be tailored so that the level of effort to establish and maintain the agreement/relationship is commensurate with the value received.

1.3 *Choosing the best tool for the job*

Contracts are often seen as negative and a source of contention and delay. This perception is valid in some cases, but it can be avoided through effective and efficient commercial management. Failure to avoid this perception handicaps the business through the loss of a critical management tool.

The problem begins with the fact that many professionals (including those in the customer's procurement organization) are intimidated by the words 'contract' or 'agreement' or 'commitment'. They believe that the creation of these documents should be left to lawyers. This approach is a recipe for disaster as it removes business people from the business document that underpins the relationship. It also frequently

leads to contract discussions being left until it is too late. The only way a contract can effectively represent and support the desired relationship is if it is created with input from the business people involved. Starting to consider and structure contract principles from the very earliest interactions not only reduces eventual cycle times, but also results in a sustainable agreement.

→ figure 1.1

Looking back at the continuum, on the left-hand side the business involvement is not intense or burdensome, even though it is important. Moving across to the right, the input from business professionals becomes critical and is often the difference between success and failure. Indeed, inaccurate or incomplete requirements and scope are the most frequent sources of contracts failing. These are closely followed by poor management of change.. Essentially, if we are unsure what we want or what we are committing to deliver, and we have not properly defined how changes will be managed, it should come as no surprise when relationships go wrong.

① 'inaccurate requirement
② incomplete requirements
③ poor change management

Developing appropriate and valuable input to contract formation is a skill that is honed throughout a business career, but lack of experience is not a good excuse for ignorance. An understanding of some basics gives anyone the chance to think about the necessary elements in the agreement.

In business, everyone is focused on their problems—competitive edge, revenues, profits, cash flow, market share, or earnings per share. Public bodies are looking to improve performance at reduced costs. Keeping that focus in mind will assist in understanding what type of contract or contract clause can help resolve the issues a customer or supplier really cares about and will help achieve a business objective. Remember both problems and opportunities, and do not lose sight of strategic issues and priorities.

Approaching this process first from a seller's perspective means that a seller must think about buyer needs. From the results of surveys done around the globe, sellers find that customers focus on three major needs.

- **Customers want to narrow their focus to the few things they do best and outsource the rest without the added overhead costs of supervising their suppliers.**

Customers

(1) focus on core capabilities
outsource the rest
&

Product-focus
↓
Value/Benefit focus

This means that the contract must also change focus from product (an input) to benefit or business result wherever it can (an output or outcome). Grandiose products and services with more capacity, features and options than required are often just seen as overpriced. Products and services must be presented as simple to use and manage, either in their own right or because the seller manages the complexity as part of the process. The focus must also change from 'price and delivery' to utility and ease of use, not only of the product but also in doing business with the seller. The seller of choice will take responsibility for managing the relationship or the 'partnership' between seller and customer.

- **Customers want their sellers to know their business well enough to create products and services they wouldn't have been able to design or create themselves.** A supplier fulfills this role by developing its business knowledge and using what it knows to identify needs and solve problems. Some ways of accomplishing this include making certain the contract achieves the following:

  - Focuses on the big picture, not just on details. An example would be to ensure that the contract addresses the regulatory environment and is not simply a pro-forma model unrelated to industry, geography or product or service specifics.
  - Identifies issues and needs at all levels (i.e., overriding business issues, organizational issues and priorities, functional issues and needs, individual issues and needs) and addresses them with appropriate terms. Although most commonly such issues may affect areas such as service levels, customers will also want to see direct incentives placed on the supplier to perform in these critical areas. This may include 'negative incentives' in the form of performance undertakings or liquidated damages.
  - Makes recommendations on the basis of the customer's long-term needs, not on just the current sale—structuring the contract and its terms to enable easy change and adaptability. A longer-term commitment will often affect the price or charging structure, resulting in the supplier sharing in risk by making recovery over time.
  - Elicits information from customers that helps define and strengthen the direction of the agreement. For example, the customer may plan overseas expansion or alliances that would

require altered approaches to licensing terms or distribution rights.

- **Customers want evidence that their supplier has added value in excess of price.** A supplier who fulfills this role coordinates all selling and service related activities and facilitates communication among the key players in the customer account team and in the customer organizations. In doing this, they should make the following recommendations for the contract:

  - Seek information and potential issues from others across the customer organization.
  - Initiate the coordination necessary to meet future as well as current needs.
  - Adopt a problem-solving and preventative approach to production, delivery and service problems.
  - Assist the contract drafters to develop best statements of the products and the added services that highlight customer value while minimizing risk.

Gathering the customer information can also help develop an adequate basis for contract recommendations. Understanding the world from their perspective goes a long way toward developing a contract that will make sense from their perspective.

 Case study: Spotting opportunity

Very Large Software Company (VLSC) was a worldwide corporation with offices and support teams in more than 80 countries. CC Enterprises (CCE) was a major customer, based in the US, but with operations in almost 200 countries.

CCE had issued an RFP to acquire more than $250 million of licensed software for use in its offices worldwide. VLSC was struggling to develop a response because of the difficulty of establishing prices in all the relevant countries and the risk that CCE would object to the price variations. So they offered to supply all the products in the US, at US prices, so long as CCE then shipped relevant materials to its overseas locations.

This solution raised many issues, including one they had not anticipated . . .

ASC was a major competitor of VLSC. They had been trying to grow their presence in CCE and had periodic meetings with the head of IT Procurement. One of those meetings occurred shortly after the deal with VLSC had been signed. The meeting was interrupted by an urgent phone call trying to resolve CCE's problems in exporting VLSC's software: "Something we aren't familiar with". The Sales Manager from ASC said: "Maybe we can help—we ship software all the time".

The result of this conversation was that ASC won a contract to manage the distribution of its competitor's product. Based on this, CCE appreciated their flexibility and commercial creativity and steadily, ASC started to win more and more business.

Approaching this process from a buyer's perspective means that new approaches must be evaluated to enhance value. Since most customers have already maximized their savings from 'commoditization', the next logical step is to look for greater value through building stronger relationships with key suppliers—but which suppliers and what kind of relationship?

Another way to think about relationships with suppliers, and thus the types of behaviors that would be most appropriate, is to assess the extent to which the supplier relationship would be suitable for partnering. Table 1.1 shows the main factors to take into account when considering partnering rather than the traditional relationship where a service is simply provided for an agreed price.

Table 1.1   Factors affecting suitability of a partnering relationship

Factor	Suitable for partnering	More suitable for traditional relationship
Strategic importance	Business critical	Support service
Benefits sought	Business value	Cost savings
Requirements focus	Outcome based	Resources based
Purchasing approach	Long-term arrangement	Standalone transactions
Payment type	Shared benefits	Fixed charges
Type of relationship	Trust	Formal
Likelihood of change	Liable to change/uncertain	Unlikely to change/stable
Definition/measurement	Difficult to define/measure	Easy to define/measure

Developing a more significant relationship requires greater initial effort and additional attention to maintain, but future synergies and harnessing the creative efforts of a suitable partner will generate higher profits for both parties.

 A contract is a business document that must make sense for both parties and cannot be created in a vacuum.

1.4 Summary

With all the changes in the way that customers view suppliers and the shifts in what suppliers of commercial goods and services have to do to get and retain business, the contract becomes more significant than ever. Flexibility in terms and conditions, creative contractual agreements, being easy to do business with—these are all areas of importance for both buyers and sellers. Effective commercial management can bridge the interests of both parties and balance rewards and responsibilities. It can also protect both parties from unintended commitments and from making agreements that cannot be fulfilled.

Checklist: Understanding the buyer's perspective

☐ Where does the item I am buying or selling fit on the relationship continuum?

☐ What is the current relationship with the vendor or customer?

☐ Is there increased value to be gained by investing in the relationship?

☐ Is there a cost or risk associated with not improving the relationship?

☐ Will changing this relationship impact other corporate relationships?

Sellers always need to understand their buyers. The following questions can be helpful to encourage thinking from a buyer perspective:

• What are the customer's business goals and objectives? Are there plans and activities taking place that support the goals and objectives?

- What are their most recent sales and profit figures? What are their trends? What is happening in the marketplace in which the customer operates? What share of the market does this customer supply?
- What changes are occurring in the customer's organization? Are they centralizing? Decentralizing? Re-organizing? Who seems to be getting the upper hand? Marketers, production people, technical people, financial people? Marketing people tend to pursue revenue, sales growth and market share. Production people focus on costs and schedules. Technical people focus on having the newest, fastest, state-of-the-art equipment wanted in their particular market. Financial people are primarily concerned with profit, return on investment and control.
- Where are existing customers located within the customer's organization? Do potential customers exist who are not being called upon? Where are these potential customers located?
- What are the customer's problems, needs and wants as related to the products and services being offered? Are the problems or needs recognized or unrecognized?
- How do specific customers within the account make purchasing decisions about what the supplier sells? How do they evaluate and rate the supplier's products and services versus direct competition or versus suppliers of alternative offerings?
- What is their decision making process? Does the process vary across customers within the account? Who is the primary decision-maker? Who influences the decision? Are influences external or internal to the organization?
- What should be learned or remembered from any previous bids or contracts with this customer? For example, are there specific regulatory issues that must be addressed in the contract? Do they have a good payment record? Do they commit the necessary skills and resources to support implementation or share in performance oversight? Are there particular risks that must be covered, or areas of relationship strength that should be acknowledged?

CHAPTER 2
ESSENTIAL ELEMENTS
OF A CONTRACT

Simplicity is the ultimate sophistication.

Leonardo da Vinci

2.1 Overview: what is a contract?

What is a contract and when does a domestic or international contract actually come into being? The answer is not always simple.

A contract is a binding legal obligation between two or more parties. It is enforceable in a court of law. All contracts involve the principles of offer, acceptance, and consideration, but the rules and principles vary from one country to another.

Basically one party makes an offer and the other party accepts it. The offer and the acceptance have to match for the contract to be formalized. In the simple snow-shoveling example the young man's act of raising his snow-shovel with a questioning look constitutes his offer. The older man nods his head as acceptance after establishing the price, or consideration.

Offer

When a potential customer puts out a request for tenders or alternatively, a Request for Proposal, he or she is inviting a seller to make an offer. When a seller issues a tender or proposal document in response, which is an offer to the customer. This tender could become the contract if it is accepted by the customer 'as is' and either:

- The customer signs it, or
- The customer places an order on the terms of the seller's offer

This is a straightforward and intentional exchange to create a contract, but many other customer interactions have the potential of becoming a contract. Requirements for a valid contract vary from one country to another. It does not necessarily have to be in writing to be considered a contract. In some countries, a contract may be established via a series of faxes, an exchange of messages between computers, or simply an oral agreement during contact at a trade fair—or even through the actions of the parties as if a contract is in place, often referred to as 'through performance'.

Acceptance

Acceptance is voluntarily agreeing to the terms of an offer and results in the creation of a contract. Perhaps the most common business scenario is the exchange of standard forms. The seller will submit standard terms of sale to the buyer who will respond with a pre-printed purchase order containing conditions. Both parties agree that they want a contract, but they do not agree as to what terms should govern. This sets up what is known as the 'battle of the forms'. If a dispute arises when there has been this type of exchange and there is no clear agreement, courts will generally rule that the last form exchanged before performance is the governing contract.

Looking at another example on the principle of acceptance, a customer sends in an order for a tractor, including its own purchase order terms and conditions. This is the customer's **offer** to buy. The seller may either ship the goods, in which case the seller has accepted the customer's offer, or they may send back a confirmation of the order, referencing the seller's own terms and conditions, in which case they have made a **counter offer.** Offers and counter offers may be exchanged any number of times until an agreement is reached.

 Scenario

A salesperson is staffing a booth at a trade fair. He tells a potential customer that his company is offering a special price on a solar powered gadget if it is ordered before such and such a date. He gives the customer a brochure. Later the salesperson finds out that the price he told the customer was wrong. The brochure had the correct price, so he doesn't worry about it. The customer sends the company an order at the price the salesperson stated, referring to their conversation at the trade show.

Is there a contract?

Maybe, maybe not. Under some legal systems, the salesperson had made an oral offer and the customer had accepted the offer under the conditions stated. If the salesperson had called the customer to withdraw (take back or correct) the offer before the customer sent the order, there would not have been a contract. In

Eastern European countries, contracts must be written documents in order to be valid. Other countries require written documents for contracts over a certain monetary value. For example, in the US, contracts worth over $500 must be in writing to be enforceable. Under most legal systems, the offer (written or oral) must be clear, definite and specific enough so that a court of law could determine the intention of the parties.

Consideration

The third element in forming a valid contract is the principle of **consideration**. This means that a valid contract must provide value to both sides. One party provides the goods and the other party pays, or offers to pay. Consideration can also take the form of some other value. In forming a joint venture agreement, one party may provide technology and a patent license. The local partner may provide land and office space, local influence and personnel. The consideration is the **value** that each party is providing.

 If the elements of an offer, acceptance, and consideration are present it is likely a contract has been formed, whether intended or not.

2.2 *Different types of agreement*

This section outlines the commonly used agreements relating to a contract:

- Non-disclosure agreements (NDAs)
- Preliminary agreements
- Sale of goods only
- Sale of services only
- Sale of goods and services
- Licenses
- Leases

More complex and specialized agreements are discussed in the subsequent section.

 Case study: The right contract saves time

One global provider of services and technology has identified eight core relationship types, ranging from a commodity sale to a joint venture. As soon as a new opportunity is identified, the sales team enters details into the Customer Relationship Management system, which automatically identifies the most appropriate contract model. The system also identifies whether internal experts will be required to support the bid and automatically alerts them to its existence. This process has resulted in an average reduction to the bid and negotiation cycle time for complex agreements of more than a third; it has also resulted in an improved project success rate of almost 25 percent.

Non-disclosure agreements

Non-disclosure agreements (NDAs) are often the first formal contractual relationship between two parties and their use has become far more extensive in the last ten years. They govern the protection of information that is shared and fall into two general types, unilateral and mutual. A unilateral form protects the information of one party and places obligations on the other. A mutual form protects the information of both parties and places the same obligations on each.

The nature and type of NDA should reflect the business needs and information sensitivities and not simply reflect the respective market power of the parties or a "we always do this" attitude. Key questions to consider include:

- What do we want/need to do with the information received?
- What do we need the recipient of the information to be able to do with it (for example, talk with potential subcontractors)?

NDAs are discussed in more detail in Chapter 10.

 Mutual non-disclosures are generally seen as more fair and balanced than unilateral forms simply because the same obligations are imposed on both parties.

Preliminary agreements

It is often wrongly assumed that the individuals involved in preliminary discussions are free to negotiate without having to worry that their actions, written communications or phone calls may have legal consequences. In fact, legal obligations can take effect in pre-contract situations when the elements of a contract are present. Similarly, these interactions may be deemed part of any eventual contract that is created. If there is an eventual dispute, all communications can become material in its resolution.

Preliminary arrangements can take many forms. From the time the initial customer contact is made until the moment a contract is signed by both parties, there are many different preparatory or preliminary arrangements that take place. These can be:

- Oral discussions or agreements
- Exchanges of information, marketing materials, product descriptions
- Price estimates
- Exchanges of letters, emails, text messages
- Memorandums of Understanding/Letters of Intent

It is important when having these preliminary discussions for both sides to be upfront and honest about their intentions, their authority or lack of authority, and whether these are exploratory discussions only. Contractual liability can arise whenever suppliers and customers exchange technical and commercial information.

Four common challenges occur during or as a result of preliminary discussions. Consider these four challenges, the type of liability that may arise in each case, and how it could be avoided:

- There may be errors in the information provided. The customer may take some action based upon the information that proves to be incorrect.
- The supplier might inadvertently make an offer, or the customer may think the supplier has made an offer. The supplier might not be able to follow through with the entire offer, or with some details of the offer.

- Either party may have no real intention of entering into a contract on the project or with this other party. Perhaps a party lacks the proper approvals to proceed. If one party relies upon the other party's representations and forgoes some other prospects, a binding legal obligation may arise, regardless of a party's actual intent.
- The customer may insert an 'Entirety of Agreement' clause into the final contract, specifying that all prior communications are material to their decision and therefore form part of the agreement. The IACCM surveys of 'Most Negotiated Terms' show that this is an increasingly contentious issue and the legal discovery process (in the event of litigation) frequently involves digging into every communication between and within the parties—so great caution is needed.

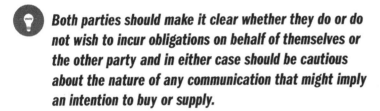

Both parties should make it clear whether they do or do not wish to incur obligations on behalf of themselves or the other party and in either case should be cautious about the nature of any communication that might imply an intention to buy or supply.

Sale of goods only

Contracts for tangible goods are generally simpler than for those involving service as well as goods or intellectual property. Purchase contracts contain three basic elements. They:

- Define what is being bought
- Specify a price and payment terms
- Outline the delivery conditions

Warranties and performance issues should be spelled out, as well as any intellectual property governed by the contract. Termination and remedies are also normally delineated. In any contract that crosses international borders, customs clearance, delivery and insurance obligations must be clearly understood. Typically the relevant internationally recognized Incoterm definition is used, which enhances clarity and avoids possible confusion. The Incoterms rules are also known as International Commercial Terms. These terms are a series of pre-defined commercial terms published by the International Chamber of Commerce. They are widely used in international commercial transactions.

As previously explained, the absence of a written agreement or of certain key clauses does not mean there is no contract or that those missing terms do not apply. The legal system within whatever jurisdiction the trade has taken place will provide the missing components, which may or may not generate a favorable result. In some jurisdictions (in particular those which follow principles of Statute Law) it may not be possible to alter certain provisions, even if both parties are willing negotiators. Most countries have specific laws that protect consumers and cannot be overridden.

 Ensure that these critical aspects are clearly defined in the contract. A person with no knowledge of the transaction should be able to pick up the contract, read it, and understand these basic facts.

Sale of services only

Services contracts have additional issues that are of importance to the buyer and the seller. In the supply of services, the contract frequently represents the only tangible item that will be delivered and establishes procedures for the delivery of services.

Service contracts can take many shapes and cover a multitude of services from office cleaning or website support to consultancy services or business process outsourcing. Their success is typically defined in terms of an output (for example, an architectural drawing) or an outcome (for example, a germ-free operating environment). A contract for the supply of services is required whether obtaining professional advice and guidance from a consultant or engaging a service provider's labor force, but is made more complicated because of the need to agree a mutually acceptable definition of 'success'.

These contracts can be relatively brief but defining certain elements is essential for an effective and efficient relationship. These include:

- Scope of the services/work to be provided
- How the service performance will be measured
- How the relationship between the service provider and service recipient will be managed

FUNDAMENTALS OF CONTRACT AND COMMERCIAL MANAGEMENT

- Timescale for performance, including handling delays
- What the charges are and how they are to be applied
- How payment will be made, specifically if it is tied to milestones
- Liability
- Intellectual property rights, if any
- Termination

Control over any engineering, development, or design is a unique issue to service contracts. These terms often vary by situation but must be considered carefully by both parties for a successful relationship.

 Service contracts define a relationship and its obligations. They will normally specify an output or an outcome that forms the basis of the value to be delivered.

Sale of goods and services

A contract for services may include products, in which case the same issues as previously discussed must be addressed. Frequently this is simply done as a matter of convenience when a single supplier supplies both products and services, but the drive for differentiation has caused many suppliers to examine their offerings and accept greater performance responsibilities by bundling both products and services into 'package' offers. This is taken a step further when 'solutions contracts' are offered, which carry substantial responsibilities for performance, interoperability of components, and suitability for the customer's end use. These arrangements go significantly beyond the scope of a simple product/services offer and are discussed in more detail under the section on complex arrangements.

There tend to be significant industry variations in the extent of 'bundling'. Some buyers push for complete separation on the basis that this increases the extent of competitive bidding.

 Combined contracts address the issues of supplying products and services together.

Licenses

Licenses are similar in many ways to contracts for the sale of goods, but the property is intangible and there is generally no transference of ownership (legal judgments have determined that there is transferability in certain circumstances). In a license arrangement the person who actually 'owns' the property grants a license to authorize a specific use by a licensee of the product. The licensor usually grants this for a specific period of time and often for a specific location, item of equipment or number of users. The license usually restricts the use of the product, especially in terms of its geography.

Intellectual property licensing has assumed a more significant role in the global economy as technology has advanced. It plays a major role in contracts beyond IT or telecommunications, because business practices such as franchising, publishing, and merchandising rely on the same principle of intellectual property protections. Equally, the extension of patent and copyright protections to business methods and processes means that businesses are now anxious to protect—or avoid breaches— in many areas of their possible activities.

Given the scale and impact of licenses, it is important to understand what happens if the license terminates either because of a breach of the license agreement, such as non-payment, or because the license period ends. Failure to understand this can have a catastrophic effect on a business if the licensed item is an essential element of the licensee's business.

 A license permits use of something but does not transfer ownership.

Leases

A lease is a contractual arrangement for a user or lessee to pay an owner for the use of some asset. It is similar to a license in that there is no transfer of ownership to the user during the term of the lease (though some lease agreements may enable transfer when they terminate, or offer a buy-out option). A lease generally provides for regular payments throughout its term and has a specific end-date. Leases are often used as a means of financing, avoiding capital expenditure or for managing tax liabilities.

The terms 'lease' and 'rent' are often used interchangeably, although a lease tends to be for a longer period, with a specified end date, and may (as noted above) lead to an eventual transfer of ownership. Leases and rental agreements generally apply to tangible property, although there are exceptions such as radio frequencies.

As with licenses, it is essential to understand what happens when the lease ends.

 Leases are commonly used in real estate and as a means of financing capital expenditure.

2.3 *Other business relationships*

A relationship between businesses does not always involve the selling of goods and services to each other. Contracts play a different role in these relationships as they define how the companies will work together, for example to either 'sell through' one another (a distribution or sub-contract relationship) or 'sell with' one another (a co-marketing agreement).

Because of this fundamental difference the terms in these contracts have significant variations from those in sales contracts. However, the key elements for these agreements still rely on a clear description of purpose, of exactly what each party will do under the agreement, of the financial commitments of the parties, and of how the success of the relationship will be evaluated.

The global nature of business today has expanded the need for agreements to sell through or with others, particularly in certain areas of the world. Many companies use agents, representatives and distributors to help in generating sales beyond their borders. Others are obliged to enter into formal partnerships or joint venture arrangements with local entities as a condition of doing business within that country. Some benefits of these relationships include:

* Familiarity with business practices, cultural customs and ways of conducting business in a particular market.

- Previously established relationships with customers to help open up sales opportunities for suppliers.
- Preference to buy from locally owned and known entities rather than from a foreign company.

However, there are also potential risks and drawbacks, which include:

- Potential for corrupt practices, such as bribery, or ownership by government officials.
- Local laws may create significant protections for an agent or distributor, making their termination difficult and expensive.
- These relationships can inhibit future freedom of action, for example if markets change or new products are introduced and require a different approach.

 Case study: Everyone has to win something

HOC was a major supplier of complex technology to the oil and gas industry. It developed integrated solutions at its consolidation centre in Houston, Texas, before shipment to customer locations worldwide.

SCC was a manufacturer of mainframe computers with a worldwide distribution network. HOC wanted to acquire SCC products in the US and, after integration, ship them to the locations of its end-user customers. It then wanted SCC to provide local support, including installation and warranty services.

This represented a major challenge for SCC. Its network of distributors provided local support and many of these contracts included undertakings that the distributor had exclusive rights to supply within their market. Although the SCC sales team initially agreed to sell the products, the local distributors refused to handle them unless they had significant compensation. It seemed like there was an impasse.

But SCC's commercial team realized that the contract structure was wrong. They advised that SCC equipment should be sent to HOC on a consignment basis; it would then be shipped by SCC as an integrated product and imported by the local distributor.

This had a further beneficial effect because total costs were reduced, on average by almost 25 percent, primarily due to reduced export and import taxes and duties. And because final sale was now by the local distributor, they were incentivised and happy to provide local support. The US Sales team lost some of their commission, but retained a valuable customer and received a bonus for their creativity.

2.4 *Complex and specialized agreements*

As business relationships evolve and become more complex, contracts tend to do the same thing. There are often very complex and specialized agreements that are prepared for unique situations, but may then find applicability in other situations and industries. Examples are shared risk agreements that found their origins in the construction industry, or agile development contracts that started in software.

Recent trends toward outsourcing have added a complexity to relationships and contracts as businesses seek to have tasks performed by suppliers that were previously done internally. The issues of service quality and control are often pitted against price and set the stage for conflict. It is not unusual for these contracts to extend for five years and beyond, and establishing ground rules is essential for effectiveness.

Outsourcing has been accompanied by a more general trend for suppliers to take greater responsibility for the performance of their products and services. Until recent times, most business-to-business contracts operated on the principle of 'let the buyer beware'. In other words, it was the buyer's responsibility to ensure that the goods or services being procured were broadly 'fit for purpose'. Of course, suppliers could not actively misrepresent their goods. But today, driven by a combination of buyer and competitive pressure, many suppliers take direct responsibility for the value that is achieved from their goods or services. For example, a manufacturer of telecommunications equipment no longer simply sells the equipment; they often sell an infrastructure service using this equipment to major telecommunications providers such as China Mobile, Vodaphone, AT&T or Telefonica.

Situations also arise where business between two companies expands in the natural course of dealings. Customers may begin as casual buyers and progress along the relationship continuum. In other cases customers may want to become dealers of a product or become a local service provider as they gain expertise. There can be a tendency to try to make a single contract serve many purposes. Occasionally this will work; but more often than not the competing interests will result in conflicting terms that leave exposure to significant risks in some area of the business.

 Case study: Acting in good faith—or not

Hungry Jack's was the largest franchisee of Burger King outside the US, operating 168+ restaurants. Over time Burger King had increased its interest in the operations of Hungry Jack's; there had been numerous disputes, which led to four new contractual agreements.

The Development Agreement required Hungry Jack's to open four new stores each year in Australia. An additional clause made the opening of any new restaurants subject to Burger King's operational and financial approval.

The disputes came to a head in 1995, when Burger King withdrew all approval for third-party franchisees, and stopped granting financial or operating approval to proposed new stores, which meant that Hungry Jack's was unable to open four restaurants per year, as required by the new agreements.

In November 1996, Burger King attempted to terminate the agreement, on the basis that Hungry Jack's had not opened the required number of stores. Hungry Jack's sued Burger King, alleging that Burger King had no right to terminate the agreement, and also challenging the validity of the new extension agreements. They argued that the Development Agreement included an implied term of good faith (that is, that the parties must act in good faith when exercising their rights under the contract), and that Burger King had breached this term by denying the financial and operating approval to new restaurants, leading to Hungry Jack's failing to meet the minimum stores requirement.

Hungry Jack's was successful at trial: the judge found that Burger King had not acted in good faith; rather, their actions were efforts to harm or hinder the other party. The judge awarded Hungry Jack's nearly $AU 71 million in damages.

 When more diverse relationships are contained in a single contract the risk increases of inappropriate and conflicting terms.

Checklist: Questions to ask about what type of 'contract' to use

Will the document being used:

☐ *Describe the transaction completely?*

☐ *Assure the customer they will get what they expect?*

☐ *Assure the supplier they will get paid?*

☐ *Provide both parties with the protection they need?*

2.5 Summary

While relationships can become extremely complex, to be effective, the contract should thoroughly address the basic business, contractual and technical elements of the purchase. In general, the more simple and straightforward the contract is, the more likely it will achieve its purpose.

Keep in mind the nature of the product or service for which the contract is being prepared. Not all situations deserve the same level of contracting. Not every contracting term applies in every situation.

CHAPTER 3
BEYOND THE WRITTEN WORD

*We are masters of the unsaid words,
but slaves of those we let slip out.*

Winston Churchill

The previous chapter outlined contract types and specified the type of information required for each to be successful and achieve the desired result. This information is explicitly stated in the contract. While clarity and completeness are essential for any contract to be effective, both buyers and sellers must be aware of the terms that apply to their contracts, whether or not they are spelled out within the documents. These terms are often referred to as 'implicit' or 'implied'.

The rules by which many contracts are governed are contained in commercial laws that deal with particular subjects. Most countries, for example, have laws that deal directly with sale of goods, lease transactions and trade practices. These laws vary by country, and while they may be similar on some issues they are by no means identical or consistent. *This means that two contracts containing exactly the same words are interpreted differently, depending on where they are performed and the laws that govern.* The difference is in the unstated terms.

As an example, a seller submits a price quotation to a customer for 30 steel machine parts, giving a 60-day period in which the offer has to be accepted. Before 30 days have passed, the currency fluctuation in the seller's country makes the offer unprofitable. Is the seller allowed to simply withdraw the offer? The answer to that question is based upon the terms that are in the contract by the virtue of law. If the contract is governed by the Convention on the International Sale of Goods (CISG), the seller must honor the price for the 60 days. If the contract is under the Uniform Commercial Code (UCC), it may be withdrawn.

This chapter will look at the commercial applications of some of these legal systems so that there is a basic understanding of the principles that go beyond the written words. Transactions that go beyond a single country are obviously more complex because there is the potential for conflicting legal systems.

This chapter relates to commercial contracts only. Specified laws and practice drive public sector and governmental contracts.

In this chapter we show charts of what can go wrong, to highlight the range of different impacts in different jurisdictions.

3.1 *Civil law versus common law*

The two primary legal systems in the world today are civil law and
common law. However, there are significant variations by country
even within this broad categorization and there are also major trading
nations that operate under neither—for example, Islamic law and
Chinese law. This is not intended as an authoritative comparison
between systems, but rather to generate awareness of the types of
differences that exist and the need for understanding of the system
that will apply to a specific contract.

Continental Europe, Latin America, most of Africa and many Central
European and Asian nations are civil law countries. Common law began
in England, and it is the system used in many of the countries that were
once part of the British Empire (these include Australia, Canada, India,
and the United States).

Civil law systems are based upon legal principles and codes rooted in the
laws and legal system of the Roman Empire. Updates to the legal code
are made through legislation or other formal process. Judges make
rulings based only on the codes and statutes. Many view this process as
more stable and representative than common law.

Common law systems are based primarily on past judicial opinions,
which are interpretations of legislation that is considered more as a
guide than a literal requirement. Common law systems acquire their
laws over time and may be changed by the ruling of a single judge.
Many consider this a more flexible and expeditious legal system than
the civil law.

An excellent example of this distinction in the commercial transaction
process is seen in the standard warranty provisions when selling goods
in Germany. Warranty in Germany is regulated by the BGB
(Bürgerlichen Gesetzbuches), which is the German Civil Code. It is a
book of minimum laws that cannot be altered. The warranty period is
clearly regulated by the BGB as being a two-year period, and
contractual provisions that are shorter are not valid. In business-to
business sales, the choice of legal forum may be changed to one more

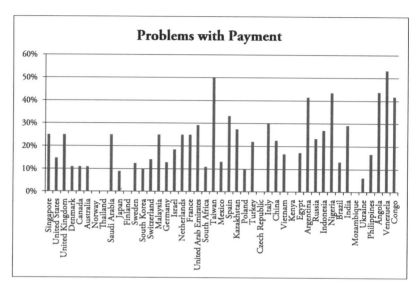

Figure 3.1   What can go wrong—problems with payment

favorable to the seller. The law of the country of the consumer governs sales to consumers. Lack of awareness of the civil/common law differences can lead to costly mistakes; German buyers will frequently state that the two-year warranty is mandatory. Unless the sale is for consumer goods sold directly to a consumer this argument may be explored for alternatives.

3.2 *The UN Convention on Contracts for the International Sale of Goods (CISG)*

Because there are so many variations in national laws relating to the sale of goods, the United Nations developed a set of rules governing international sales. This is referred to as the UN Convention on Contracts for the International Sale of Goods (CISG). The United Nations Commission on the International Trade Law (UNCITRAL) developed the CISG. At the time of publication CISG has been accepted by over 75 nations, including most of the major trading nations (except the United Kingdom).

 Business people **must** *understand that unless the parties specifically indicate that CISG does not apply to the contract, the CISG will be the governing law for any commercial contract for the sale of goods between parties having their places of business in different countries that have adopted the CISG.*

Unlike civil code provisions, the parties may agree to terms that directly conflict with the CSIG, as long as that agreement is clearly written in the contract. For example, if the parties do not agree to the contrary, a commercial sales agreement between a business in Monrovia and one in Toronto (both Liberia and Canada having adopted the CISG), will automatically be subject to its provisions. However, if the parties wish to be bound by some other law, such as the UCC or Ontario sales law, they may opt out of the CISG by specifying that the other law will apply, as well as stating that the CISG will not apply.

The parties cannot, however, change the law to provide for something that would violate any other laws, local, state, provincial or national. They cannot contractually avoid certain liability such as product liability or liability for death or personal injury, although they can provide limits on either party's contractual liability to the other party.

The CISG permits contracts to be formed by an exchange of purchase orders that are accepted or confirmed through the exchange of forms containing conflicting small print terms. This happens quite frequently between parties in an international transaction. Under the CISG, an acceptance that contains modifications is considered a rejection of the offer, and constitutes a counter-offer, unless the modifications do not materially alter the terms of the offer and are not unacceptable to the offeror. If the offeror does not object verbally without undue delay, then the contract terms become those of the offer, as modified by the acceptance.

This means that the small print terms of an acceptance or order confirmation are binding unless promptly objected to, or unless they constitute material changes to the offer, or purchase order, with respect to price, quality or dispute resolution.

This is known as the 'battle of the forms' under both common law and civil law.

The CISG preserves the buyer's right to sue for breach of contract. However, the right to 'avoid' or terminate the contract and reject the goods is quite limited. The buyer may reject goods and require delivery of substitute goods if the contract has been 'fundamentally breached'.

In general, however, the CISG allows the seller who fails to perform on time, or who delivers nonconforming goods, to correct the performance as long as it does not cause the buyer an unreasonable delay or inconvenience. In addition, the buyer can also avoid the contract if, after notifying the seller to perform the contract within a reasonable time, the seller refuses to do so. This is a novel remedy in common law.

The CISG also gives the seller protection against the potential financial failure of the buyer. The seller may, by sending appropriate notice, suspend delivery or prevent the release of goods if it becomes apparent that the buyer may not have the ability to pay for the merchandise. The seller must continue with delivery if the buyer then provides adequate assurance of payment.

The CISG is based partly on the common law tradition, but is also influenced by civil law and socialist law. Socialist law is very similar to civil law, and is the legal system of communist and former communist states.

The CISG governs only the formation of the contract of sale and the rights and obligations of the seller and buyer arising from such a contract. The CISG is not directly concerned with the validity of the contract, where a person is induced into a contract by fraud, where a person does not have the capacity to enter a contract, or where domestic law prohibits the sale of goods specified in the contract.

The CISG promotes freedom of contract over the regulation of private international behavior. It allows business people to operate more

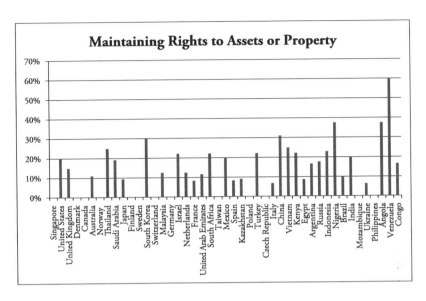

Figure 3.2   What can go wrong—maintaining rights to assets or property

efficiently in the growing international marketplace. A table showing the countries that have signed the CISG is in Appendix A.

3.3 *The Uniform Commercial Code (UCC)*

The system used within most of the US is the Uniform Commercial Code. It is a 'model code' or example, which means that it has no legal effect in a particular jurisdiction unless the legislature has enacted that particular statute. Currently the UCC, in whole or in part, has been enacted with local variation in all 50 states, the District of Columbia, and the US Virgin Islands. The goal of the UCC is to harmonize state laws to facilitate commercial sales transactions across state lines.

The overriding philosophy of the UCC is to allow people to make the contractual agreements they want, but to fill in any missing provisions where the agreements they make are silent. For example, the UCC contains warranty provisions that any items sold will be fit for sale and also fit for their intended purpose. These warranties apply unless they are specifically excluded.

The UCC also seeks to impose uniformity and streamlining of routine transactions such as processing of checks, notes, and other routine commercial papers.

The UCC and CISG are similar but not identical. Some significant differences that are frequently seen in the commercial transaction process are:

- The UCC requires all contracts of more than US$500 to be in writing. The CISG does not require the agreement to be in writing in order for it to be an enforceable contract.
- In the UCC, an acceptance of an offer containing non-material different terms and conditions still operates as an effective acceptance. Under the CISG, most non-conforming acceptances (having different or additional terms) will automatically be considered counter-offers.
- All terms relating to price, payment, quality and quantity of goods, place and time of delivery, liability and dispute resolution are deemed to be material terms. Therefore, a contract will not exist until agreement is reached on all material terms.
- Under the UCC, it is presumed that the offer is not firm (may be revoked, taken back) unless it is specifically stated that it is irrevocable. Under the CISG, stating a time limit in which the offer must be accepted creates a firm or irrevocable offer.

The UCC is the default governing law for interstate sales of *goods* within the US. By contrast, the law governing the sale of *services* in the US is common law, which varies more widely from state to state or country to country. Most standard service terms and conditions, in addition to covering issues not relevant to the sale of products/systems, also take the differences among the laws of the various states or countries into consideration.

3.4 *European Union (EU) law*

Under European Union (EU) law parties are free to enter into a contract and to determine its contents, subject to the requirements of

good faith and fair dealing, and the mandatory rules established by a set of Principles set out in *The Principles of European Contract Law 1998, Parts I and II*.

Either of the contracting parties may exclude the application of any of the Principles or deviate from or vary the Principles' effects.

Under EU law the intention of a party to be legally bound by contract is to be determined from the party's statements or actions, as the other party reasonably understood them. EU law also states that if one party refuses to conclude a contract unless the parties have agreed on some specific matter, there is no contract.

Contrary to contract law in common law countries, EU law states that contract terms that have not been individually negotiated may be invoked against a party who did not know of them only if the party invoking them took reasonable steps to bring them to the other party's attention.

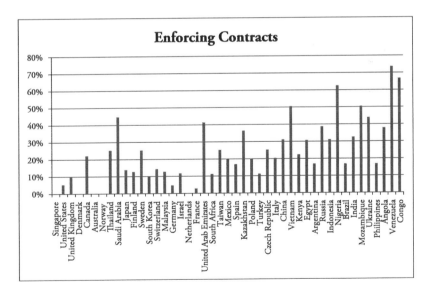

Figure 3.3   What can go wrong—enforcing contracts

3.5 Private commercial law

Certain industries have developed specific standards for contracting, which in a few cases have evolved into a system of private law. Many argue that keeping disagreements out of court is more efficient and less costly, especially for international transactions. Indeed, even the courts increasingly push businesses to undertake arbitration or mediation before litigation.

The use of model agreements is especially common in industries such as construction, engineering or oil and gas, even though there are often conflicting models (e.g. FIDIC, NEC, JCT).

Examples of those who have opted out from the public legal system are still relatively rare, though the cotton industry and the international gem trade are two.

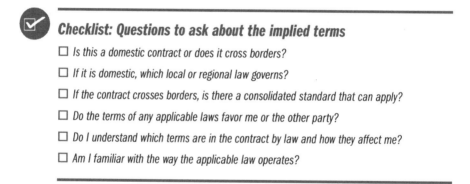

Checklist: Questions to ask about the implied terms

☐ Is this a domestic contract or does it cross borders?

☐ If it is domestic, which local or regional law governs?

☐ If the contract crosses borders, is there a consolidated standard that can apply?

☐ Do the terms of any applicable laws favor me or the other party?

☐ Do I understand which terms are in the contract by law and how they affect me?

☐ Am I familiar with the way the applicable law operates?

3.6 Summary

Not all contract terms are spelled out in the documents themselves. There is a wide range of laws that fill the gaps when terms are not specified. It is vital for the business professional to understand which terms are present by operation of law as well as which terms can be negotiated. Detailed interpretation of the finer points resides appropriately with legal professionals, but everyone involved in contract development or delivery should have a good foundational knowledge of the principles.

CHAPTER 4

COST, PRICING, AND PAYMENT

What is a cynic? A man who knows the price of everything and the value of nothing.

Oscar Wilde

Virtually all commercial transactions are more complex than the introductory snow-shoveling example. In global markets, much greater analysis is given to costs, price, and payment, especially in the context of the relative severity and impact of risk.

4.1 *Customer perspective on costs*

The customer's starting point is their business case: a requirement has been identified, with needed business benefits, and initial approval obtained for the project. The customer must now gain a realistic understanding of the likely cost of the project and the associated risks.

The complexity involved in calculating the investment cost varies directly with the complexity of the project. For example, the simple replacement of an item of office machinery should be easy to quantify: the cost of decommissioning the existing equipment, the cost of purchasing a new item and the cost of installation, plus the cost of after-sales support and relative reliability and performance. But in a situation where the equipment replacement is part of a major update involving changes to workflow processes, there will be the costs of process redesign, staff training and perhaps changes to supporting systems and services. It may be necessary to produce return on investment (ROI) calculations over a period of several years and these must take account of the probability and consequence of disruption or failure.

Risks relating to a specific project will vary a great deal, depending on complexity, sensitivity, uncertainty and many other factors. It is important to note that the customer's perception of a risk and a supplier's perception of the same risk are not necessarily the same; the key consideration will be the extent to which either party feels it can control the risk and the costs placed by each party on managing the risk.

The contract is the vehicle used to allocate risk. Decisions must be made early in the process on where the buyer and seller want the risk to be. The ultimate decision will be made as the contract is negotiated. That risk is then managed through the effective oversight of the contract as it is implemented.

Some useful tools and techniques for customers to evaluate costs include Monte Carlo simulation (to create cost scenarios with different cash flows) and the Balanced Scorecard (to link business objectives and desired outcomes from the investment in the project to future performance). Further information on these can be found in a variety of general business books.

 Controlling and managing risk—and where responsibility for this will lie—is a major determinant of cost.

4.2 Basic pricing principles

Many factors affect a supplier's pricing of products and services. The impact of different international laws and currencies is perhaps felt most acutely in this area. Regardless of location the primary factors in any pricing decision are basically the same:

- What are customers willing to pay?
- What are the supplier's competitors charging?
- What are the supplier's costs involved in the sale?
- What pricing or charging options are available and affordable for the supplier?

 The most important factor is what the customer is willing to pay.

Beyond these basic factors, depending on the particular market, there are many other contributing considerations. The key issue is to understand what the supplier is trying to achieve in this market.

- The supplier may be trying to develop a permanent market position to realize long-term profits from expected growth.
- The supplier could be seeking higher short-term profits in a market where there is some uncertainty about a continued commitment.
- The supplier may be seeking to defend, maintain or grow market share in an established market.

- The supplier may be introducing a new product or offer that has considerable economic value to a customer.

What the supplier is attempting to do will largely influence whether it sets moderate prices, which may not generate much initial profit, or higher prices, if market conditions will allow them. Alternatively, it may actively use a new charging or pricing model as a source of competitive differentiation, particularly where this positively impacts the financial or risk factors for the customer. These were the drivers behind initiatives such as outsourcing, software as a service and financial leasing.

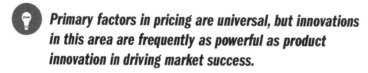 *Primary factors in pricing are universal, but innovations in this area are frequently as powerful as product innovation in driving market success.*

4.3 *Legal considerations*

Government price controls
Governments in developing countries sometimes employ price controls as economic policy instruments. This can take the form of freezing the prices of selected products or a blanket control that may affect industrial and technical commodities. Price controls are more likely to occur with frequently changing or unstable governments and following high inflation and severe economic difficulties. For example, price controls in Brazil in 1990 resulted in sharp reductions in earnings for a number of US-based companies operating there. Some measures that various companies use to combat price controls include negotiating with the government for exceptions, preemptively raising prices, modifying the products or associated terms and conditions to reduce their cost or provide barriers to their export, or making them not subject to controls.

Anti-dumping laws
Government controls apply not only to the upper end of a pricing range, but also to the lower end. The purpose of anti-dumping laws is

to prevent predatory pricing where foreign-made products are being priced so low that they pose a serious competitive threat to domestic producers of similar products. Countries that have anti-dumping laws may prohibit imported goods from being offered for sale at prices below their presumed cost of production or below the price charged for the same goods in the company's home market. If the government thinks that a company's pricing practices may be causing economic injury to local producers, it can assess higher import duties or impose other penalties. Such cases are often referred to the World Trade Organization for resolution.

 Example:

Anti dumping laws could become an issue for a company in connection with its subcontractors or suppliers. For example, if a Korean company were to sell an American company subsidiary in Venezuela a semiconductor for use in a major local project, and there were Venezuelan manufacturers of semiconductors who claimed they were being undercut in price, the American company might be subject to penalties or restrictions imposed by the Venezuelan government.

Some countries may require pre-shipment inspections to verify that the quality, quantity and price of purchased goods do not violate anti-dumping laws. Many developing nations, such as Indonesia and the Philippines, hire inspection companies to ensure that imported goods are properly valued. A company commonly used to conduct such inspections is SGS (formerly Société Générale de Surveillance). The inspection process includes a physical examination of the goods at the exporter's convenience. If SGS suspects that the local government is not getting its fair amount of Customs and Import Duties due to under-pricing of the goods, the goods will be held up in Customs. Exporters do not have to wait for SGS to contact them. They can request a physical inspection in advance by providing relevant details in writing.

 International law affects even transactions that are considered 'local'.

4.4 *Factors that influence pricing*

Competition

The competition that a supplier faces is the major factor capable of putting both upper and lower limits on its pricing. If a supplier prices too far below its competitors, it may stir up antitrust concerns or be perceived as having lower quality products. If it prices too far above its competitors, it may be pricing itself out of the market. It is important for a supplier to understand exactly what its competitors are including in their prices so that it can differentiate itself based on value factors other than cost.

Variable cost pricing

Many companies dealing in developing and developed markets adopt a strategy of marginal cost or variable cost pricing. This means that the price of a product may not fully cover the costs of producing and distributing it at a given time, largely due to high initial costs or start-up costs.

Inflation

All companies must adopt pricing tactics to compensate for inflation in the countries in which they do business. In developing countries, rates of inflation have historically been much higher than in more mature industrial economies.

The effects of inflation include increases in the prices the supplier must pay for labor and services as well as impact to cash flow and profitability. However, depending on the origin of the goods, these increases may be offset by a change in currency exchange rates. Where possible and practical, pricing should be based on the cost of replacement of the products currently being sold, rather than on historical costs.

Currency fluctuation is tied to inflation and affects the pricing decision. Agents and distributors may want to specify a percentage of fluctuation that may occur before prices and commissions must be renegotiated. Currency fluctuation should be considered when issuing prices that are valid for any extended period of time. It should also be noted that high-inflation countries often also impose strict exchange controls, limiting the repatriation of profits. This has driven many companies to explore extreme tactics to continue doing business in these markets. For

example, at one point a Fortune 25 global technology company acquired equity positions in domestic hotels in a South American country that restricted capital repatriation; this enabled the company's capital to work while waiting for economic stabilization.

When structuring or negotiating a final price, suppliers need to be sure that they have looked at all of the following and included them as part of their cost structure, if applicable:

- Credit investigation expenses
- Commissions and other costs for agents or representatives involved in the sale
- Special manufacturing costs
- Product modification and special packaging
- Shipping costs
- Freight forwarder fees
- Special export documentation expenses
- Customs duties and taxes that will not be reimbursed
- Translation costs
- Banking charges
- Insurance (casualty/credit)
- Financing costs
- Foreign exchange hedging costs
- Standby Letter of Credit
- Fees for bid and performance bonds or guarantees
- Consulate and other government fees
- Legal fees

In addition, the supplier will have to factor in the potential costs of any extended warranties, post warranty support services, or increased liability exposure.

 Case study: bid to win, but not at any cost

An Ottawa company, Corporate Research Group Ltd (CRG) was fined $125,000 in 2012 after pleading guilty to a criminal charge of bid-rigging. CRG had made a secret agreement with First Porter Consultancy of Ontario to bid together for a major contract to provide real estate advisory services to the Canadian federal government.

Canada's Competition Bureau launched an investigation after the Department of Public Works and Government Services Canada alerted it to the possibility of bid-rigging following a request for standing offers for real estate advisory services. The Competition Bureau team noted several similarities between the bids during their investigation. The two bids combined would have given the companies 80 per cent of the department's real estate consulting work.

CRG officials admit that they and First Porter Consultancy submitted co-ordinated bids under an agreement that was not disclosed to Public Works. Under the Competition Act, it is a criminal offence for two or more bidders to agree among themselves on the bids submitted, to agree that one party will refrain from bidding or to agree to withdraw a submitted bid, without informing the party calling for the bids of this agreement.

This does not necessarily mean that the final price will reflect all of these costs. For reasons of competition or with the expectation of getting future profitable orders, a supplier may decide to price below the fully loaded cost of a contract. Very often, the overriding factor is what the customers are willing to pay. But at least suppliers should have a complete knowledge of what those costs are, so that they have a solid basis for their pricing decisions.

 The most important factor in pricing is to relate product or service value and the proposed price or charge structure to what the customer is willing and able to pay.

4.5 *Pricing models/contract types*

There are many different types of contract pricing arrangements in use today. By far the most common fall into a category of firm fixed price or fixed price units. There are many types of cost reimbursement contracts, but these are more commonly found in the public sector and place an enormous accounting burden on suppliers.

In today's competitive environment, suppliers are being forced into more creative and flexible arrangements to meet customer budgets and needs. The approach to pricing (or charges, in the case of many services or licenses) has a major effect on contract terms and risks. For example, until relatively recent times, most contracts involved full payment for goods at the point of delivery. Today, many of those product sales have become subject to agreements where payment may be phased and depends on performance. Often they are part of a long-term services agreement or an outsourcing arrangement. This means that the supplier has residual responsibility for the output or the outcome that is achieved, fundamentally altering the term, duration and conditions of contract, as well as the supplier's cash flow and funding requirements.

The following is a discussion of a multitude of pricing arrangements that are sometimes used. These do not include the various financing options that may be available—for example, renting, leasing or securing third party funding.

Firm fixed price (FFP)

This contract type requires the delivery of specified products and/or services at a specified price, fixed at the time of contract award and not generally subject to any adjustment.

Fixed price with economic price adjustment (FPEA)

This is a contract type that fixes price but allows escalations based on specific criteria for periods after the initial term. The contract must contain a clause explaining how the price adjustment will be made, identifying the price index to be used, the frequency of adjustment, and any overall ceiling price.

Fixed price incentive (FPI) or shared benefits

This is seldom used because of the high cost of administration and difficulty in performance evaluation. It provides incentives for efficiency in performance by increasing the percentage of fee for exceptional performance. Many customers who indicate an interest in such a formula during the bid process actually change their minds when it comes to the final contract, partly because their budget systems cannot easily deal with the uncertainty of this formula.

Firm fixed price, level of effort (FFPLOE)

This type of contract is useful in some cases when selling professional services. It provides a specific number of hours for a stated period of time at a fixed price.

Time and materials (T&M)

In this type of contract labor rates are fixed for specific categories and other direct costs or materials are billed directly, usually with no fee added. All profit or fee on labor is built into the rate. There is sometimes a price ceiling that the supplier exceeds only at its own risk.

Time and materials labor-hour (T&M LH)

Labor-hour contracts are a type of time and material contract differing in that the supplier does not provide materials, so the contract is for labor hours only.

Cost sharing (CS)

This type of contract is similar to cost reimbursement; it provides for sharing of costs between the customer and the supplier, rather than full reimbursement of cost.

Cost plus fixed fee (CPFF)

In this contract type, an estimated cost and fixed fee (profit, stated in a specific dollar amount) are negotiated at the time of award. Costs are reimbursed up to the estimated cost and the specified fee is paid. The fee does not change, regardless of the costs incurred; it may only change when the customer directs a change in the work to be performed. This contract is appropriate for use only when no other type of contract would work.

Cost plus incentive fee (CPIF)

This type of contract reimburses suppliers for costs incurred and then a formula is applied to determine the appropriate fee.

Cost plus award fee (CPAF)

This contract combines elements of the cost plus fixed fee and cost plus incentive fee by providing an estimated total cost (costs are reimbursed), a minimum fee, and an award fee based on the quality of the supplier's performance.

Exclusive requirements/indefinite delivery (ID)

An exclusive requirements contract provides for the purchase of all actual needs of the customer from one supplier for specific supplies or services at fixed prices during a stated period of time. There is a realistic estimated total quantity, but no guaranteed minimum, and purchase orders are issued to obtain the needed items.

Indefinite quantity (IDIQ)

This contract type works in the same way as the requirements type contract, except that there is a guaranteed minimum that the customer must order (either in dollar terms or number of units). The contract generally also contains a ceiling on the total amount that may be ordered.

Commitment contract

This contract is similar to the requirements and indefinite quantity types. It is used when the customer knows the precise quantity of items needed, but there is uncertainty as to when delivery is required. Consequently, this contract provides for a specific quantity of supplies or services to be purchased, but delivery orders specify the quantities and times of delivery within the specified total.

General purchase agreement (GPA)/basic ordering agreement (BOA)

A GPA (also known as a **framework**) is not a contract. It is an agreement that provides terms and conditions that will apply to future contracts or orders during a specified period of time, a description of the supplies or services needed (as specific as practicable), methods of pricing and issuing orders, delivery terms, and a statement as to when any subsequent order becomes a contract.

 Every contract pricing and payment type has risks and rewards and should be matched with a suitable requirement. Discussions about price should never be divorced from wider considerations of contract terms because they are interdependent.

4.6 *Estimating and job costing*

To establish the supplier's contract baseline, and to establish the final price, the supplier must come up with an accurate and reasonable cost estimate. Contracts for the sale of off-the-shelf goods are easy to cost, but special custom design and manufacture is much more difficult. The hardest to estimate are those involving consulting, design, construction or installation (services). Aside from the obvious hard costs associated with construction or installation projects, there are many hidden costs that can occur. Poor estimating and scheduling are two of the biggest causes of project failures.

Tracking costs and projecting final costs during the course of a construction or installation project is vital for the supplier who wants to be paid for all of their work. Aligned with a good schedule, tracking and projecting costs forms the basis of what is needed in managing the job, the customer, and the profits. The natural outcome is projects that are completed on time and within budget.

 Effective cost estimating and tracking lead to better project management.

4.7 *Payment management*

When companies sell goods or services to customers, one of the most critical aspects of the sale is analyzing the customer's ability and willingness to pay for the goods or service. In some cases, especially in unfamiliar or overseas markets, there may be both commercial and political risks that could affect a supplier's ability to collect on the sale. Some of these risks are:

- Customer insolvency—not enough cash/heavy debt
- Limited foreign exchange availability
- Import license cancellation
- Debt rescheduling
- Political instability

- War
- Cultural attitudes toward due dates and banking procedures

Because of possible risks in doing business with some customers, it is important that a supplier completely evaluates this risk with all new customers and each new contract. When the supplier has enough information to determine what the risk is, they can then decide on the appropriate customer payment terms and methods of ensuring payment.

Many suppliers have corporate resources that can perform the following analytical services and recommend the appropriate type of payment terms for a particular customer:

- Credit and financial analysis
- Country risk analysis
- Standby Letter of Credit and surety bond negotiations
- Bank negotiations
- Open account collections
- Documentary Letter of Credit negotiations
- Third party or parent guarantee
- Results analysis

It should be noted that many of these mechanisms are also used or demanded by customers. They frequently have parallel concerns about the long-term viability or commitment of their supplier, especially if the contract creates any form of dependency on the supplier. Hence they will be undertaking regular reviews of credit and other risk and may seek performance guarantees or bonds to ensure that the supplier meets its commitments.

 Correctly analyzing a customer's ability to pay is vitally important.

4.8 *Main types of payment*

Payment terms are an issue of great sensitivity because suppliers want to ensure they are paid and customers want to ensure they obtain value before payment. The topic has been made more complex by the introduction of legislation covering Revenue Recognition, which makes a supplier's ability to book revenue contingent upon the payment terms. In addition, large customers have increasingly extended the period for payment, which today averages 57 days after delivery, and have introduced incremental terms such as taking discount for 'early payment'. Some countries (for example the EU) have enacted legislation to protect small suppliers from the unilateral actions of large corporations, and governments (for example the UK) have implemented policies requiring their departments to pay within 30 days of invoice.

These factors combine to make an understanding of payment term options and behaviors of great importance when reviewing, constructing or negotiating a contract.

Open account

A high percentage of the world's business is conducted on 'open account'. This means that the goods will be shipped and/or the services will be performed before any payment or guarantee of payment is made. The supplier invoices the customer and expects payment in 30, 60 or 90 days, depending on what has been negotiated. Of course, offering extended payment terms will adversely affect the profitability of the sale and must be considered in the pricing decision.

The supplier generally uses open account payment terms only with customers who have been pre-qualified as posing a very low risk to the supplier's company. Many distributors are billed on 'open account' terms.

Open account is the least secure method for getting paid and should only be used with trusted customers with whom the supplier has had experience or when there is no risk. Open account terms are widely used in the UK and the US with 30-day payment terms.

Cash in advance

This method is probably the most secure method of making sure that the supplier gets paid, if the supplier can get the customer to agree to it. The customer makes an advance payment of a specified percent of the contract value. Unless protected under local law, an advance payment generally needs to be secured by an advance payment bond that the

supplier has to obtain. These protect the customer. After the goods are shipped or work is completed to an agreed upon point (either a specific milestone or final delivery), another advance payment may be made. No interest is paid on advance payments. These payments are applied to the customer's invoice.

Many customers will not agree to advance payments, so the supplier has to look at other alternatives. However, it is not unusual to have some form of phased payment in major capital projects or complex developments of customized goods or services. This is essentially a risk-sharing mechanism in circumstances where the supplier is making substantial investment, much or all of which could not be recovered from other customers,

Personal or individual guarantee
This is a legal document making the principal of the customer's organization personally liable for payment to the supplier, in the event that the company or organization fails to make payment.

Corporate guarantee
Some smaller customer companies with an inadequate credit rating may be affiliated with a parent company that has an acceptable credit rating. In such cases, the corporate parent may agree to guarantee payment.

Irrevocable Standby Letter of Credit
Issued by the customer's bank, this is drawn upon only if the customer does not make payment. This approach is used more frequently with international customers.

Purchase Money Security Agreement (PMSA)
Used primarily with resellers or distributors in the US, this legal agreement gives the supplier a security interest in the inventory shipped. It is negotiated through an outside agent. For standalone transactions, a UCC-1 document will serve the same purpose.

Consignment sales
In some circumstances, a supplier may make sales 'on consignment'. This allows their customer to delay payment for a certain period or until specified conditions are met. It is used most frequently in

distribution relationships, where a third party representative is selling the goods to an end-user. However, it may also be used in situations where the goods are sub-components of a final assembly or product, for example in the aerospace industry.

 Matching payment to the risk of collection is done through specifying payment terms.

4.9 *Standard Letters of Credit*

Commercial or documentary Letters of Credit

This type of Letter of Credit represents a guarantee for both the buyer and the seller. If the use of a Letter of Credit is agreed to by both the supplier and the customer, the customer applies to its bank (the issuing bank). The customer's bank has to approve the customer's credit and then issues the Letter of Credit that describes the documents required and the payment terms.

The Letter of Credit is then sent to the supplier's bank of choice, called the advising bank. The advising bank checks to be sure that the Letter of Credit is authentic and delivers it to the seller.

Standby Letter of Credit

A Standby Letter of Credit is a simple, less expensive alternative in some cases. The customer opens a Standby Letter of Credit. The seller would draw under a Standby Letter of Credit only if the customer fails to pay outstanding invoices within a specified period of time. As with the Commercial Letter of Credit, the issuing bank is obligated to pay, provided the terms of the Letter of Credit are met. Standby Letters of Credit are useful in projects requiring regular transactions or multiple shipments, such as with distributors.

Collections/Bills of Exchange

Collections (also referred to as Bills of Exchange) are similar to Letters of Credit but the supplier's bank does not bear responsibility for assuring payment. The bank acts as an agent to forward the documents to the customer's bank and make presentation for payment. These offer less protection to the supplier but there are several advantages.

- The supplier or its bank can (if it chooses to) retain title and control of the merchandise until the buyer has paid.
- Collections are far less likely to have errors in the documents than Letters of Credit.
- Both banks (the supplier's and the customer's) work for the supplier.
- The customer's failure to pay does not affect the supplier's legal rights to pursue collection or the supplier's credit insurance.

 __Letters of Credit can be extremely expensive to obtain and while this may be considered part of the 'cost of doing business' eventually someone pays that cost.__

4.10 Bonds

In addition to the various guarantees of payment the supplier requires from its customers, the customer may also require guarantees of performance from the supplier. These take the form of several different types of bonds issued for the supplier in favor of its customers.

Bid bonds

These are usually required in accordance with the customer's tender document (invitation to submit a bid). The purpose is:

- To guarantee that the supplier will accept the job and honor the contract if chosen as the successful bidder.
- To assure that the supplier's bid is in 'good faith'.
- To assure that the supplier will post a performance bond.

Bid bonds are generally from 1 percent to 10 percent of the value of the bid. The term or validity period of the bond is usually the time period that the bid is valid, but can be extended at the request or demand of the customer. If the supplier is chosen as the successful bidder, they must keep the bid bond active until a contract is signed and a performance bond is posted. If they are not chosen as the successful bidder, the bond will be returned.

Performance bonds

These are also required by the tender and are usually from 5 percent to 10 percent of the contract value, but could range as high as 100 percent.

The performance bond takes over after the contract has been signed and replaces the bid bond. This is to make sure the supplier performs as agreed to in the contract. The term of the performance bond is either receipt of an acceptance certificate for the job, or acceptance date plus any warranty period. The customer can often extend performance bonds upon demand.

Advance payment bonds

We mentioned these earlier. These are required only if the supplier receives an advance payment on the project. The value of the bond matches the value of the advance payment, usually 10 percent to 20 percent of the contract value. This bond can be extended or called in by demand of the customer. Advance payment is common in the Middle East.

The form of all of the above bonds can be either:

• A Standby Letter of Credit issued by a bank
• A bank guarantee, issued by a bank in the customer's country, backed by a bank's Standby Letter of Credit
• A surety bond, issued by an insurance company

Which type of bond is used will largely depend on the customs and culture of the country. Most of Latin America prefers to use surety bonds, while Europe, the Middle East and Asia generally use bank bonds.

These bonds can be very costly to the supplier. The supplier does not have much choice as far as these required bonds are concerned. They are a cost of doing business. The costs must be considered and factored in to any decisions on pricing or profitability of the contract. US banks charge commission rates of from ¼ percent to ½ percent per year. Banks in other countries will also charge commission rates. These can be from ¾ percent up to 6 percent of the value of the bond in countries that have cartel arrangements for bank services (such as Turkey). A supplier has to pay both parties' bank charges.

Warranty bond

If the supplier agrees to provide an extended warranty, the customer may request a warranty bond to cover the period of the extended

warranty. This is a negotiated item and not standard procedure. If the supplier does agree to extend the warranty, they must consider the cost of this bond in addition to other costs.

 Bonds are costly, and may make it difficult for a supplier to identify revenue for a sale. Eventually someone pays the cost.

Checklist: Cost and pricing questions to ask

☐ What is the customer willing to pay?

☐ What price do competitors charge for comparable product or services?

☐ What are the costs to produce the item or provide the service?

☐ What type of contract is best suited to the project?

☐ Is the customer able to pay? Is the supplier able to deliver?

☐ Is a payment or performance guarantee necessary?

☐ How will we pay for any required bonds?

4.11 Summary

Cost, price and payment analysis cannot be done in isolation from risk analysis. The risk of doing any particular transaction will be reflected in the price, and the contract vehicle chosen could either increase the risk or help to manage it.

The business objectives of a supplier influence price. The price of a product in a well-established market might vary substantially from the price when a supplier is trying to gain market share. Inflation and currency fluctuations must not be ignored when setting prices that will be fixed for a length of time.

Suppliers always have concerns about a buyer's ability to pay. Buyers have concerns about a supplier's ability to deliver. Both sides address these concerns by structuring payment methods and terms as well as guarantees of payment or performance such as bonds and letters of credit.

CHAPTER 5
NEGOTIATION PRINCIPLES

It's learning how to negotiate to keep both sides happy—whether it's for a multi-million dollar contract or just which show to watch on TV—that determines the quality and enjoyment of our lives.

Leigh Steinberg

Negotiation is a business process. Some feel it is shrouded in mystery. Other people fear it and feel only experts or those specially trained are qualified to do it. Many feel it is a game and keep a score. Despite these different perceptions, negotiation is simply another business process that is improved with a basic understanding of the procedures involved, planning for effective execution, and integrating the business information and goals of the specific situation.

 The primary purpose of negotiation is to reach an agreed position acceptable to all relevant parties.

Like every other business area, there are people who specialize in negotiation and for a number of them it may form a significant portion of their professional duties. Negotiation, however, does not only exist in this realm. Every person is, at some level, a negotiator, both personally and professionally. Negotiation is part of the fabric of daily life.

This chapter is not meant to transform readers into professional negotiators. This chapter intends only to demystify the process and provide some guidelines for planning and tools for integrating business information and goals into practical negotiation results.

This chapter does not wrestle with the thorny issues of what we should negotiate. Those issues are covered later in Chapter 15 after specific contract clauses have been discussed. This chapter focuses on the negotiation principles of 'how'. It is essential to remember that effective negotiation depends on mastery of both elements: what and how.

5.1 *Negotiating approaches today*

The purpose of negotiation is to reach consensus, but that does not mean all negotiations are collaborative or marked by mutual concessions. Indeed, in the business world, negotiations may be quite adversarial, and the more powerful party will frequently create barriers to change or compromise.

In 'Getting to Yes', one of the best-known books about negotiation, the authors developed a distinction between 'positional' and 'principled'

POSITIONAL	PRINCIPLED
Low value/importance (to them)	High value/business significance
Wide choice/competition	Limited choice/competition
More powerful	Less or similar power
Unempowered negotiator	Empowered negotiator

Figure 5.1   Positional and principled negotiators

approaches. The positional negotiator is someone who seeks to achieve his or her goals at the expense of the other party. The principled negotiator seeks to understand the interests of the other side and to reach conclusions that are of mutual benefit. These two approaches typically generate quite different outcomes. For example, principled negotiation is typified by the trading of value and often produces a result that exceeds the expectations of both parties (a 'win-win' solution), whereas in positional negotiation, it is more likely one party will feel they have 'lost' and in consequence, they will be less committed to the agreement.

While theories and observations of books such as 'Getting to Yes' are useful background, today's business opportunities are seldom presented in clearly defined scenarios that can be resolved with a standard or singular approach. Most negotiations are a mix of the positional and the principled.

5.2   *Negotiation styles*

This book uses the 'continuum' concept to describe business relationships and transactions. Negotiation styles tend to run along a continuum as well (Figure 5.2). Both principled and positional negotiating styles have their places in business, and many negotiations involve both approaches at different phases. If you have the luxury of choice, the selection of one

Figure 5.2   Negotiation strategy continuum

style over another should be conscious and based on the transaction and the business relationship that exists or is desired.

In a recent large outsourcing contract, the Australian Department of Defence conducted the initial negotiation under the typical 'positional' style of most public procurement. But once the contract was signed, it engaged in a further negotiation that was highly principled in nature. This second negotiation was to agree upon a collaborative framework for contract and performance management in which both parties agreed the detailed framework for the management of their relationship.

At the extreme left of the continuum is a style that is labeled as 'concessionary' because the party that employs it makes all of the concessions during the negotiation. This produces an outcome of 'lose-win' where one party sacrifices so the other party can profit. The opposite end of the spectrum is the 'competitive' style where every point is highly contested and considered almost a prize. Not surprisingly this produces a 'win-lose' outcome that is the opposite of the concessionary approach. The closer the two parties are to cooperation, or the middle of the continuum, the more collaborative the approach and style will be. This collaborative style produces a 'win-win' outcome.

The more important an ongoing trading relationship is, the more the negotiation will be driven to the middle of the continuum. Single transactions, particularly those not requiring respect of the other party, tend to drive behavior to the two extremes.

Regardless of the underlying psychology, the important thing is to understand the continuum. Knowing and understanding one's personal comfort zone on it and determining the zone of the other party is vital. *The ability to move across the continuum as needed to resolve the business problem is critical to successful negotiation.*

The importance lies not in accurately labeling a particular approach, but in understanding how to most effectively achieve the business objective. It is here that negotiation strategy comes into play.

Thinking of negotiation as another business process can be helpful to remove anxiety from those who have not been involved with it

professionally. Like other processes, there is no set amount of time allotted to negotiation. All of the steps may be completed in a single day with one phone call and a few emails, or it may take several months and a string of calls, emails, and meetings.

A negotiation generally moves forward in four loosely defined stages, as shown in Figure 5.3:

- Stage 1: Orientation, planning, and positioning
- Stage 2: Argument, compromise and search for alternative solutions
- Stage 3: Emergence and crisis
- Stage 4: Agreement or final breakdown.

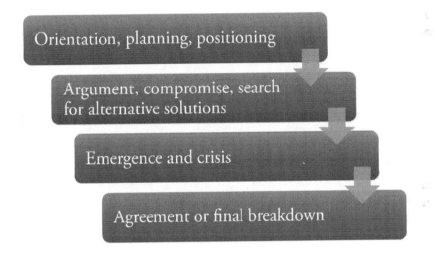

Figure 5.3   Negotiation stages

Stage 1: Orientation, planning, and positioning

Negotiating teams must establish the 'rules of the road' to define how they will work together. This includes establishing whether they have the expertise to resolve issues and the authority to make decisions that are required.

In many situations the process will begin with the exchange of standard terms and conditions, often in the form of pre-printed contracts.

A review of the standard or desired terms by the other party enables an assessment of how closely the two parties are aligned on the approach to the project. If it has been previously determined that the standard terms of one party will be used, the other party will review those standards and prepare a list of issues or concerns that it would like to see changed in the final agreement.

A review of this type establishes the general scope of the negotiation. Both parties understand what the issues are between them, and they can then plan the steps needed to resolve them. It is at this point that the negotiators are able to determine if specialists need to be involved to suggest alternatives or approve changes. This preliminary work significantly reduces the time spent later in the process.

While no one can predict how long a negotiation will take, a review of the issues can help the teams determine a proposed plan for the negotiation. There should be a general plan for how the discussions will be handled—conference calls, web meetings, or face-to-face meetings. If additional individuals need to be involved to resolve specific topics, their availability should be arranged. It can often be helpful to have specific goals for a meeting, especially if the negotiation is long or complex.

Meetings should be scheduled to support any significant dates or required events. If an item being purchased must be received by the end of the month, postponing negotiations to the last week does not support the desired result.

Setting expectations for the negotiation ensures the teams are aligned. This can be as simple as an email stating the teams will meet for a one-hour call at 10:00 on Tuesday to discuss insurance requirements, payment terms, and delivery. It may be as complex as a detailed schedule of calls, meetings, and document exchanges involving different teams for specific issues. Each negotiation is unique. Both parties should agree to the planning, commit the necessary resources to be available, monitor the progress and raise alerts if necessary.

The final step in this stage is presenting the initial negotiating position. It can be difficult to assess what the initial position should be. A collaborative strategy generally challenges negotiators to establish a range

or zone within which both parties can reach an agreement. Individuals most often consider this concept as relating to cost or price alone; however, the concept also applies to any issue within the contract. For example, there are many variables in an area such as payment terms; or the assignment of liability is not simply 'either a or b' but a wide range between the two that can be explored for agreement.

Further guidance on the specifics of planning is contained in Section 5.4 below. It is a key element of negotiation success and should be considered separately from the overall process.

Stage 2: Argument, compromise and search for alternative solutions

Once positioning has been determined, either through document exchange or conversations, the teams must decide on the best approach to reach an agreement.

At this stage supporting points and information are developed and issues are framed to be as persuasive as possible. Both sides are tasked with presenting arguments in a way that will be most favorable or compelling to the other side.

This can often be an education process, particularly when the two parties are from very different industries. Sharing the business case (both the presentation and the financial model) will often be the first step in the negotiations. Many aspects of this will have been raised during the previous stage and there may be indications about how much flexibility there is to move away from these initial positions.

The tendency in many negotiations is to focus only on price or what can be given away, whereas it should be on locating areas of importance to both sides and examining how they might be 'traded' for something that is of lower value. Exploring these alternatives allows both sides to look for the best options possible and emerge feeling that they have each gained.

The search for alternative solutions can help each side achieve its goals while avoiding undesirable alternatives. For example, a construction firm wanting to buy computer equipment may initially request a performance bond because it wants to ensure project completion, and that is a common requirement in its industry. The computer supplier may be reluctant to do that because of the substantial cost for what it views as a short period of performance. An alternative solution may be structuring payment terms such that a substantial payment is due only after final delivery. While this may not be ideal, it meets the objectives of both parties and may resolve the issue without further expense.

Stage 3: Emergence and crisis
After having explored the alternatives, the parties are working on converging into some sort of 'final stance'. Both parties have a better view of the positions of the other and an understanding of areas where compromise is possible. While these are not final positions, they serve as a barometer to see whether convergence can be achieved.

At this point in the negotiation process, there is often significant pressure to simply conclude the process. This pressure is felt on both sides, and crisis should be anticipated. This can be intensified if there are external factors coming to bear on the process—such as the end of a fiscal year, the need for a delivery, or an ancillary project ready to begin. Formulating a summary of the current status and evaluating the benefits for both parties can assist to defuse the crisis by providing accurate information and a realistic assessment.

Any outstanding issues should be identified and agreement pursued wherever possible, even if it is only a partial agreement. The final task in this stage is to work on each issue to devise an appropriate and satisfactory approach to reach agreement.

Stage 4: Agreement or final breakdown
This is the most difficult time in the negotiation. Each side believes it has given everything possible and that it received little or no satisfaction from the other party. It seems that no one can do more, whether financially or technically; but if the deal is to be done, then a way out of the deadlock must be reached.

The first step is to think back to Stages 2 and 3 to revisit the stakes.

- What are the stakes for each side?
- What are the elements that are most valuable for each side?

- What happens if no positive outcome is found?
- What are the concerns that have been expressed during the crisis phase?
- What conditional agreements have been obtained?

The second step should be a brainstorming within the team to address each concern and make a decisive move forward.

Finally, think of what can be traded in exchange for the concessions that are needed. At this stage, focus on those concessions that are most costly to your counterparty, hence showing that it is really a major final effort and that each party has to play its part to reach a positive outcome.

Frequently what is needed is financial creativity: ways to spread costs over a period of time, financing solutions, discounts in the form of loyalty schemes or any other solution that makes a proposal more attractive from a purely financial point of view.

Once it has been determined how to best present the results of the brainstorming, it is time to go back to the negotiation table and present the final proposal.

The outcome is straightforward:

- Either the parties come to a basic agreement
- Or it turns out that what you have come up with proves to be insufficient and this is the end of the story.

Wrapping up

The last and final stage is to write down the agreed contractual terms, making sure that they truly reflect everything that has been conceded. This is actually a very important phase as either party may forget what the other party has previously agreed during the numerous negotiation rounds.

There are practical logistics to consider at this point. If the negotiation is being done via conference call, the person drafting the final document may want to end the call with a brief summary of the changes they will make to the document and indicate when it will be sent for review and signature. If it is a face-to-face meeting it should be decided if the changes will be drafted immediately and the meeting reconvened for signature or whether the document will be prepared and sent at a later time. The shorter the period of time between the negotiation and the signature the better. Immediate signature may not be possible if there is a requirement for signature by a corporate officer or there is a need to apply a company seal or 'chop'.

All parties to the negotiation should be clear on the form the changes will take. They should understand whether changes would be made within a standard agreement or whether they will be made in an addendum to that agreement. Additionally it can be helpful to indicate exactly how many documents will be included in the final package (e.g. two copies of an order form, service terms, and statement of work) so that there are no surprises on either side. If changes are made to an existing and on-going relationship, both parties should be aware of the timeframe when changes will be made.

Wrapping up a negotiation that failed to end in an agreement is equally important. Documenting the issues that resulted in the failure helps companies understand the cost of certain policies and their impact. It can help to avoid future negotiations that are likely to have the same result. It can even lead to exploring new alternatives that might prevent a similar negative outcome in the future.

 Case study: Understanding local culture

The negotiation team at Company L was working on a supply contract that had real potential. It was with an assembly plant in the Middle East, but the team had no experience of doing business in the region. They spent time preparing for the meeting with the customer and agreed outline terms and fallbacks, including a bottom-line price. However, they did not gather data about the specific market and had only limited insight to the customer's negotiation style.

When they reached the customer premises, they were welcomed and initial discussions went well. However, after two days, they were stuck on the question of

price. The team from Company L had reached their bottom-line and had no further concessions to make. It was time to decide—walk away, or breach the bottom-line and explain to management? The team decided to walk away.

On the flight back home, the team felt dejected about their failure. However, on landing, they discovered an email from the customer saying: "We accept". They had failed to grasp a fundamental cultural issue, which was that continued negotiation meant that there was more flexibility. Only by walking away had they demonstrated that the last offer truly was final.

5.4 *Negotiation planning and strategy*

There are two extremes when looking at negotiating strategies. These are simply zero-sum negotiation and cooperation. Zero-sum negotiation is frequently emotionally charged, personal, and combative. This is the type of strategy that results in a common negative perception about negotiation in general. Cooperative negotiation looks for common interests, creating added value and establishing a transparent and trusting environment.

The diagram of negotiation strategy (Figure 5.4) looks rather different from that of negotiation style.

Both extremes on the outside are zero-sum negotiation where there is a fixed 'pie' of some sort that is divided between the two parties based upon the negotiation. The more successful negotiator ends up with the bigger piece of the pie. The cooperative negotiation strategy focuses on using common interests to expand the total pie, resulting in larger pieces for both parties.

Figure 5.4   Negotiation strategy

This is not a theoretical argument or approach. MarketWatch Centre for Negotiation reported that in its studies[1] of over 25,000 negotiators, almost half of the total potential value of a transaction is lost because the negotiators failed to explore partnerships and create added value.

'Must-have' elements

A significant element of negotiation planning is determining the elements that must be achieved in any agreement. These 'must-haves' may be a corporate imperative (eg arbitration instead of litigation), a financial objective (eg pricing), or regulatory requirements (eg data protection). Whatever the sources of the 'must-have' list, every negotiator must know and understand these elements.

Corporate imperatives often reflect corporate culture and industry norms. There are significant accounting requirements related to recognizing the revenue from software sales, and most companies in this industry will have imperatives that address the issue. It may take the form of insistence on certain warranty or payment terms or the refusal to make representations about future product availability. Corporate culture may dictate requirements for selection of consultants, dispute resolution procedures, or the requirement for status reports.

The restrictions that are created may be due to regulatory conditions— for example laws relating to bribery and corruption, data privacy or export regulations. They may be needed to protect core assets, for example licenses or patents. They may be driven by revenue recognition guidelines to preserve the integrity of financial disclosures. Unfortunately for today's negotiator, jurisdictions increasingly compete for rules and sometimes seek to 'outlaw' the rules of another jurisdiction. For example, there is recent US legislation that bans US air carriers from complying with European carbon emission laws. Negotiators must be aware of these constraints on negotiation and the fact that they vary between industries and jurisdictions.

The goal of this type of preparation is to avoid pointless negotiations. Senior executives may complain: "Why is it that I have to spend so much time explaining EU data protection laws to my US and Indian

---

1. http://www.forbes.com/sites/keldjensen/2012/02/23/whats-your-negotiation -strategy

suppliers?" but it is a typical indicator of when negotiators fail to understand the regulatory environment of their customers or suppliers. Proposed contracts either fail to contain necessary terms or are non-compliant with the law. *As regulators become more pervasive, this need to ensure understanding of your counter-party's business environment becomes more and more important if we are to avoid low value, frustrating negotiations.*

Understanding these issues from both perspectives is critical because the other negotiating party may face similar types of constraints. It is pointless to drive demands for negotiation in areas that are clearly outside the power of the negotiators to grant or discuss.

These terms are essentially non-negotiable and the size of the list varies, both by country and by industry.

Framing

The next step in preparation is *framing.* This is about organizing, shaping and focusing the information to be presented in negotiation. Framing is a perceptual process where we are trying to make sense of complex situations, in ways that are meaningful to us and that will have the greatest likelihood of achieving our desired outcome.

 Case study: The difference framing makes

A large car manufacturer has recently been hit with a number of economic difficulties; it appears that three plants need to be closed and 6,000 employees removed from the payroll. The vice president of production has been exploring alternative ways to avoid or mitigate this crisis. She has developed two plans:

Plan A: This plan will save one of the three plants and 2,000 jobs.

Plan B: This plan has one-third probability of saving all three plants and all 6,000 jobs, but has a two-third probability of saving no plants and no jobs.

Another way of presenting the plans (or framing them) could be:

Plan C: This plan will result in the loss of two of the three plants and 4,000 jobs.

Plan D: This plan has a two-thirds probability of resulting in the loss of all three plants and all 6,000 jobs, but has a one-third probability of losing no plants and no jobs.

In this example the facts in the two sets of alternative plans are identical, but the information is framed differently. The first situation has a positive framing, 'a sure gain,' and in situations like this the majority has a tendency to be risk-averse and will go for plan A. The other situation has a negative framing, 'a sure loss', and this will trigger our preference for alternative D, a possible chance of saving all jobs.

While some people dismiss framing as a mere exercise in perception, it has a significant tangible impact on negotiations and is often the strategic part of communication. It is important to analyze the situation to find the important issue, and work out how best to frame and present the information.

In negotiation both parties have frames. If the frames match, the parties are likely to focus on common issues and be united in seeking resolution, but if the frames do not match the communication can be difficult and divisive.

As negotiations evolve the perception of a situation may change as new perspectives are brought into the negotiations. This re-framing may be intentional or it may emerge from the conversations.

Establishing goals

A significant element of preparation is *establishing goals*. The negotiation team must define the goals it wants to achieve. Goals should be specific and realistic targets, not wishes that could be fantasies. In the process of developing goals it might be clear that some can be achieved through a single negotiation session, while others require a series of meetings where things can develop incrementally.

In establishing goals, it is also important to determine fallbacks and who has authority to use them. Fallbacks are acceptable alternatives to the standard or starting position that is being presented and are fundamental to negotiation being meaningful. Good negotiators do not view these as compromises or concessions; they understand that fallbacks are bargaining chips that they exchange for something that they

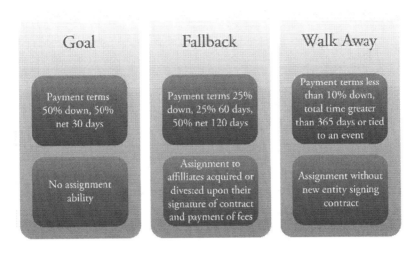

Goal	Fallback	Walk Away
Payment terms 50% down, 50% net 30 days	Payment terms 25% down, 25% 60 days, 50% net 120 days	Payment terms less than 10% down, total time greater than 365 days or tied to an event
No assignment ability	Assignment to affiliates acquired or divested upon their signature of contract and payment of fees	Assignment without new entity signing contract

Figure 5.5   Goal, Fallback and Walk Away

value. The negotiator must understand the potential connection between goals and their value relative to each other. For example, if there are alternative positions on a warranty term, the start date of the contract and the payment period, it must be determined which has the greatest value or importance.

Finally, the team must know when it is time to walk away—what is the bottom line? Without consensus in this key area, the other party has no way of knowing whether the team is serious and will most likely keep pushing for additional concessions.

Developing a strategy

After deciding on goals, the next step is ***developing a strategy*** for the negotiations. A negotiation strategy should be a plan, which specifies the choices a negotiator will make in every probable situation. The strategy is intended to integrate goals, targets and actions into a cohesive whole.

Choosing a strategy forces negotiators to balance the substantive outcome at stake in the negotiation that must be weighed against the longer-term relationship.

Often when deciding upon a strategy, an organization has a unilateral approach, pursuing its own goals and focusing on the desired outcome. In negotiation it is essential to consider the other party's interests or motivations, including their level of commitment, because the main foundation for negotiations is the extent to which there is mutual dependence.

It is important to consider what each party has at stake in the negotiation. It is important to know what happens on each side if there is no agreement. The book 'Getting to Yes' defines this with the concept of 'BATNA'—the Best Alternative to a Negotiated Agreement.

Understanding variables

As both sides present issues or perspectives, it should be remembered that this is an information-gathering opportunity. It is organizing the puzzle pieces before putting together the picture. The different variables are generally divided into four types:

- The ones important to you as they drive your costs/benefits ('driving variables'). You get those by a thorough financial analysis of your proposal.
- The ones that may look very attractive to the other party, but do not represent a high value or a high cost to you ('attractive variables'). You get those by listening actively and patiently to your counterparty and asking the right questions at the right time in a structured way.
- Tangible benefits—those benefits that are readily quantifiable in financial terms.
- Non-tangible benefits—those benefits that are not so readily quantifiable but which may still add value for one or both, such as being a launch partner of a new technology or protecting or enhancing market reputation.

 Case study: Tangible or intangible benefit?

Is reducing risk a tangible or intangible benefit? Since the probability and consequence of risk are frequently hard to evaluate in specific economic terms, risk reduction tends to be one of those intangible values that often frustrates

negotiators. Customers obviously care about their overall 'cost of ownership' and suppliers often seek to establish competitive advantage through claims of superior after-service support, relative reliability of product or service delivery or even areas such as cost of disposal. The problem is that these claims can be hard to validate.

SKF, a large engineering solutions company, has been at the forefront of establishing industry benchmarks that allow presentations showing true 'total cost of ownership'. In negotiations, their teams have genuine benchmark data rather than general claims and assertions. This has provided a real source of competitive difference, which allows the conversation to move away from price and to focus on total cost.

Once the variables have been identified, future scenarios and possible trade-offs should be anticipated, keeping as many attractive variables as possible while knowing that these should be traded against elements that are highly valuable.

5.5 *Integrating information for results*

This book focuses on obtaining information from trading partners. It is intentionally filled with questions for readers to answer, either about their trading partners or their own organization. Taking this information and creatively combining it with appropriate alternatives, variables, and fallbacks leads to a contract that can be implemented successfully and achieve objectives.

The effort involved in this step is not for every transaction. Most of the time negotiation is focused on reducing price or cost of ownership for the buyer, and profit and risk for the seller. However, there can be other, even more powerful motivators, and when these are present there are significant opportunities.

For example, most large companies use a standard software package to handle their accounting and business operations. The same package, or a similar one, is likely to be in use by their direct competitors. The ways in which a company implements or customizes the software is often believed to give them a competitive advantage.

This type of software customization has significant drawbacks:

- It is expensive
- Difficult to find competent programmers
- Expensive to change and maintain as the standard product advances
- Takes a lot of time

For these reasons customers really want their personal enhancements made to the standard product. They do not, however, want competitors to have access to those enhancements.

Software companies will not generally do custom programming such as this unless they own the code and have the right to put it into their products, because their core business is developing, marketing, and selling software.

This set of facts does not seem to offer much in terms of compromise, because both parties want something the other views as core to its business success. Many custom software development projects leave one or both sides dissatisfied because each side focuses on what it 'must have' which is usually viewed as the ownership of the software code itself. However, as the case study shows, there is another way.

 Case study: Negotiating a mutually beneficial deal with a custom software project

Bringing in specialists with knowledge of the industry and programming allowed Company A (the customer) and Company B (the software developer) to achieve more than they ever anticipated. Company A did have an excellent application of the standard product with a few modifications. The cost estimate for Company B to do the work was $250,000, or half of what an outsider would cost. They could complete the job in three months. This left Company A with only two issues: maintaining the code and protecting competitive advantage.

Company B recognized an incredible application that would have broad appeal outside Company A's industry. Using their own developers they knew that the program would be easily integrated into the standard product if it were as effective

as hoped. They would also have a live site to test the software. They could not give ownership of the code to Company A, but they could protect the proprietary nature of the idea.

The two parties chose a time window of five years—an eternity in technology. They would handle this development project in a unique manner for that period. The customer would pay $250,00 to develop the enhancement, and it would be completed within three months. Company B would have the freedom to enhance their product with the code, but would not market the enhancement to Company A's industry for the five years. However, they were free to market to other industries. Company B agreed to make any enhancements required to the custom product for five years at no cost. If the custom code was placed into the generally available product Company A would receive a credit of $125,000 to be used for either additional programming or software maintenance.

Integrating the business information gave both sides what they needed at a lower cost.

Understanding the relationships among contract clauses gives the negotiator greater flexibility to achieve objectives while still satisfying corporate and regulatory constraints. If a customer insists on a warranty that begins after installation, but a vendor insists it must begin upon delivery because of accounting requirements, the deal should not simply die. A negotiator can see the issue is only warranty for the length of time of the installation. Determining that length of time, calculating the cost of the additional warranty period and agreeing how to cover the incremental cost achieves the desired result. Simply arguing the point brings no solution.

 ### Checklist: Negotiation questions to ask

☐ *What is the main objective I am trying to achieve?*

☐ *What is the best vehicle to negotiate? E-mail? Phone? Face-to-face?*

☐ *Is there a realistic negotiation schedule?*

☐ *Are expectations in place for each session?*

☐ *Are the right people involved from both sides?*

- ☐ Is there an event on the horizon that is going to move this to a crisis point?
- ☐ Do I know the 'must haves' for my side? The other side? Is this feasible?
- ☐ Could the issue be framed so it is more attractive to the other side?
- ☐ What are the goals?
- ☐ Do I understand my fallbacks?
- ☐ Do I know when I have to walk away?
- ☐ Are all of the variables correctly identified?
- ☐ What is the alternative if we fail to reach agreement?
- ☐ What are the underlying issues of disagreement?
- ☐ Can clauses be integrated to reach solutions?
- ☐ Have I effectively documented the resolution, regardless of its success?

5.6 Summary

Looking back at the snow shovel example, we do not find the absence of negotiation. Instead, it is an example of two parties with a common frame of reference that placed a realistic value on the service being bought and sold. We talked earlier about the unspoken, almost unconscious evaluation that each one did. The negotiation could have escalated here. The man held up 10 fingers, but the young man could have shaken his head and responded by holding up ten fingers twice over. In our example they chose simply to agree.

Sometimes business is like that, but most times it is not. More often readers will be required to go through the negotiation process, with varying degrees of analysis and preparation, to achieve goals. Thoughtful use of business information obtained throughout the transaction process can achieve outstanding results.

CHAPTER 6

OVERVIEW OF THE CONTRACT MANAGEMENT LIFECYCLE— A STRUCTURED APPROACH

When one has finished building one's house, one suddenly realizes that in the process one has learned something one really needed to know in the worst way— before one began.

Friedrich Nietzsche

This chapter describes the five phases of a commercial transaction and shows how the foundations for successful operation of the contract are laid down incrementally through the phases. For a point of clarity, many books focusing on sales skills break the process into four stages: pre-sale, sale, implement, and contract close-out. We are taking a slightly more detailed approach that is convenient for both buyers and sellers.

Another way to look at the commercial transaction process is as a contract management lifecycle. The contract management process reflects and adds structure to the business process. It serves to provide a sequential framework through which the business can flow. The five phases we will examine are: Initiate, Bid, Develop, Negotiate, and Manage. These are shown in Figure 6.1 below.

Figure 6.1   The commercial transaction process or contract management lifecycle

As previously illustrated, the reality of business today is that situations move and change rapidly; they seldom flow neatly through any workflow scenario. Clarity in communication is often a casualty when speed, business pressures, expectations and change all collide in the transaction. The rush to 'just do the deal' can mean that essential questions are not asked or that incorrect information is assumed.

 Contract management imposes a structured approach to the process to ensure not that a deal gets done, but that a deal that is understood gets done.

6.1   *Initiate phase*

The Initiate phase is foundational, as many basics for a successful commercial relationship are laid down in the Initiate phase. In some

aspects it is the most 'generic' of the phases, with many of its outcomes related to several transactions rather than just one specific transaction. Of course there are always strategic situations that merit new analysis, and re-examination for competitive advantage.

This phase ensures that all members of the transaction team understand the markets and their interactions with business needs and goals. It is at this point that contract terms, structures, and practices should be aligned with those business and market goals to ensure the overall efficiency and effectiveness of the transaction process.

In the simplistic example used in the introduction, this phase would include the young man recognizing the opportunity the weather and his snow shovel provide or the older man looking out of his window and wondering how his walkway would get cleared.

This phase covers a wide range of preliminary activities involving many business sectors. These activities may include:

- Understanding markets and industry
- Understanding requirements
- Financial considerations—understanding cost and setting charges
- Aligning risk through financial modelling
- Identifying routes to market
- Preparing Requests for Information (buyer)

Questions to ask during the Initiate phase

☐ Are we taking the right route to market, including understanding our competitors? Does this opportunity fit with our business strategy?

☐ Are the outline costs and benefits agreed upon?

☐ Do we have internal/external authority to move forward?

☐ Have we identified the major risks and can we manage them?

☐ Are the scope and goals clear and unambiguous?

☐ Are the requirements clear and realistic?

☐ What access will we have to the other side, to discuss and resolve issues?

☐ Will the process present barriers to open communication and understanding?

☐ Do we have the capabilities to deliver the requirement, including our supply chain?

☐ Can we confirm our planning assumptions, including timescales and our current capacity?

☐ Is there a clearly defined project structure to pursue this opportunity?

 Without understanding and alignment among team partners the competitive advantage gained through using the right contract for the task is lost.

6.2 Bid phase

The Bid phase covers the bid process and is typically more structured than the Initiate phase, particularly in the realm of public contracting. We will explore the basic bidding and proposal activities taken by both the buyer and seller to determine the extent of the 'fit' between needs and capabilities.

The example in the introduction covers this as the buyer and seller make eye contact, the shovel is raised to indicate the services to be performed, and the price is proposed.

The Bid phase covers the bid process and the rules that apply:

• Request for Proposals preparation (buyer)
• Responding to a Request for Information or Request for Proposals (seller)
• Understanding the influence of laws on the bid process
• Costs identification
• Opportunity evaluation (seller)
• Proposal preparation (seller)
• Evaluating the proposal (buyer)

 Questions to ask during the Bid phase

☐ Are the customer's requirements clear and unambiguous?

☐ Are responsibilities clearly understood and appropriate?

☐ Are we using the right pricing models that make us competitive and commercially viable?

☐ Are we being realistic about our capability and capacity to deliver, including our supply chain?

☐ Do we have the commercial expertise to understand the customer's capability to succeed with this project?

☐ Do we have a realistic project plan that runs through to completion, with the right people in place?

☐ Have we got adequate financial controls, funding and resources? Can we confirm stakeholder authority/commitment for the whole project?

If there is no match between needs and capabilities there is probably not a profitable business relationship to be developed in this opportunity.

6.3 Develop phase

This phase is normally where the final form of a contract will be determined. The previous steps have all provided information that enables the team to proceed with the best options for a successful agreement.

Think again about the introductory example. It may seem that there was no development involved, but at some point both the buyer and seller had to determine the most effective way to accomplish their respective goals. The young man had to decide whether to charge a fixed price or charge by the hour. The older man had to decide whether the best way for him to get his walkway clear was to hire the young man or wait for a contractor with liability insurance in case of a fall.

The Develop phase covers:

- Understanding contract and relationship types
- Understanding contract terms and conditions
- Understanding specialised technology contract terms and conditions
- Understanding term linkages, managing cost and risk

- Statement of Work and Service Level Agreement production
- Following guidelines for contract drafting

Questions to ask during the Develop phase

☐ Can we confirm that the opportunity is still worth pursuing, now that we have detailed requirements/proposal information from the customer?

☐ Are we following the right pursuit strategy, in line with legal requirements?

☐ Have we assessed the impact of relevant international law?

☐ Can we make use of existing frameworks, where relevant?

☐ Can we work with the draft contract?

☐ Are the customer's terms and conditions acceptable?

☐ Do we need to review our terms and conditions?

☐ Have we got sound plans for managing service delivery, risk and change that are understood and agreed across our supply chain?

☐ Do we have the expertise and resources to manage the commercial relationship?

Understanding all of the options enables the choice of the best one for the job.

6.4 Negotiate phase

Negotiating is central to the commercial transaction process. Experts in many disciplines have written countless books with different approaches to negotiation, though these tend to concentrate more on *how* to negotiate than on *what* to negotiate. They often ignore the realities of the business world, with all its rules, procedures and fragmented authorities. This book draws from that expert body of knowledge, but pays greater attention to the practical issues and challenges that are encountered on both sides of the negotiating table.

The negotiation in our introductory example was minimal. The young man had established a fair price in his mind and proposed it. The older man evaluated the proposal and felt that the services were defined well

enough to proceed and the price was reasonable. He nodded his agreement to the young man, who started work.

The Negotiate phase covers:

- Understanding the objectives of negotiation
- Selecting appropriate approaches to negotiation (win-win, win-lose)
- Applying appropriate negotiation styles (principled, positional)
- Applying negotiation techniques
- Closing the deal

Questions to ask during the Negotiate phase

☐ *Do we understand our negotiation position?*

☐ *Do we understand the other party's negotiation position?*

☐ *Have we got the right negotiation strategy to achieve our goals?*

☐ *Is this strategy compatible with the way negotiations will actually be conducted—for example, face to face or through virtual meeting?*

☐ *Can we reach agreement on fundamental issues such as:*

  — *The Statement of Work or Service Level Agreement*

  — *Testing and acceptance criteria*

  — *Ownership of assets such as intellectual property*

  — *Managing inevitable changes*

  — *Resolving disputes*

  — *Contingencies and risks*

☐ *When do our obligations to each other end?*

Plan the negotiation to know what must be achieved to consider the transaction to be a success.

6.5 *Manage phase*

This phase moves into actual performance. The challenge here is to successfully deliver what has been planned and negotiated in the previous phases, or to manage mutually agreed changes to those plans. Different approaches can be implemented to ensure successful implementation and management of the agreement. It is the evaluation in this phase that determines whether or not the results envisaged at the beginning of the process have been achieved, or perhaps even exceeded.

In the simple introductory example we see the young man shoveling the walkway, going to receive his payment, the older man reviewing the job done and paying for the services. Perhaps, if expectations were surpassed, there will even be an additional payment or gratuity for exceptional service, or an enterprising young man will ask if he can return after the next snowstorm.

The Manage phase covers:

- Transition
- Managing risk and opportunity
- Managing and monitoring performance
- Program and project management
- Change control and management
- Dispute resolution
- Contract close-out and lessons learned

 ### Questions to ask during the Manage phase

☐ Is the business case for the project still viable, from our sell-side viewpoint?

☐ Is this a good fit with our business strategy; benefits being achieved; costs and risks as expected?

☐ Do we have a contract that is complete, up to date and aligned to current objectives?

☐ Who owns the contract?

☐ Are responsibilities clear and communications effective?

☐ Have we got enough resources to manage and perform the contract, with continuity of key personnel on both sides?

☐ Are the administrative aspects working well?

☐ Are payment arrangements working?

☐ Looking to the future, do we have mechanisms that support continuous improvement and motivate the parties to actively seek new opportunities?

☐ Do we have plans in place for evaluating lessons learned and establishing future targets?

☐ Do we understand contract closure/completion and any continuing obligations?

💡 *Every transaction teaches lessons. Evaluation helps us to learn what to repeat and what to avoid. Without it we are doomed to make the same mistakes.*

6.6 Summary

The five phases of the commercial transaction process provide a structured framework to ensure that all the tasks necessary for success are completed. This approach also facilitates communication and the sharing of information across business disciplines, further enhancing the probability of commercial success. Each of these phases will be explored in greater detail in Part Two.

💡 **To fully achieve the benefits of effective Contract Management, ALL functions that touch the Contract Management Lifecycle need to contribute.**

PART 2
THE CONTRACT MANAGEMENT LIFECYCLE

CHAPTER 7

INITIATE PHASE: REQUIREMENTS

Details create the big picture.

Sanford I. Weill

This chapter explains why requirements are important to both buyers and sellers. It describes how customers develop requirements and highlights the common pitfalls they face. It also outlines the Request for Information (RFI) and provides guidance on initial evaluation of opportunities. This chapter is written primarily from the purchasing viewpoint but will conclude with a seller perspective on requirements.

7.1 *The importance of requirements*

Requirements and contracting strategy must be aligned at the outset. The benefits of robust, detailed requirements include achieving a better solution, lowering costs, and improving implementation and adoption. Deficient requirements, or contract terms that do not support and motivate their achievement, can lead to wasted time, high levels of frustration, a decision to proceed with the wrong solution, or ultimate failure of the project.

 The number one factor to improve contract performance is improving the quality of requirements.

In many cases, achieving full understanding of business requirements or exact alignment of buyer needs and supplier capabilities is impossible. So some deviation from requirements is to be expected; choosing the closest fit and establishing a relationship that will accommodate change will achieve the best possible outcome. In this case, the purchasing team needs to prioritize requirements so that key criteria are met; the selling team must do likewise. Indeed, in situations where innovation is a goal, the contract may need to be based on very general requirements that envisage 'what' is to be achieved without either side knowing 'how' to achieve it. These situations demand a distinctive approach, often known as 'agile contracting', which assumes frequent change as a fundamental element of the relationship and accepts that the ultimate vision may not be achieved.

The requirements do, of course, include the functional and technical aspects of the particular solution being purchased. There will also be a host of other matters to be taken into account in determining the best fit, such as:

- Timescales for implementation
- Cost of solution (external—paid to suppliers)
- Cost of solution (internal—purchaser's resources required to make it a success)
- Legal and contractual risks
- Technical and implementation risks

7.2 *Developing effective requirements*

For major projects, requirements definition is a process rather than an activity. This means that it should be managed with key milestones to enable those involved to determine whether they are making progress, and how close they are to a 'good' set of requirements.

Identify the stakeholders

The first step in gathering requirements is identifying the stakeholders. If you get to the end of a project and discover that a key stakeholder has been left out of the process, the project is already in danger of failing. Even if, by good fortune, the needs of this stakeholder have been catered for, they will often present a continuing challenge during deployment of the solution because they will not have been part of the process.

Do not continue to the next milestone unless you have a high degree of confidence that you understand who the stakeholders are, what perspectives they bring and how those will be accommodated.

Understand the business objectives

Once you know the stakeholders, the next milestone to be achieved should be to understand the business objectives for the project. What does the business want to get out of this acquisition? For example, is it about streamlining processes, increasing productivity or increasing margin?

To meet this milestone you must have a clear understanding of the business objectives and these should be:

- Unambiguously documented
- Widely reviewed
- Signed off by all the stakeholders

A green light at this stage ensures that all stakeholders know why they are engaging in this project and that their objectives are aligned with corporate objectives. If there are problems with objectives (e.g. not affordable, adding complexity), ensure that executive support is clear before proceeding. Appoint a requirements group or committee if necessary to ensure that everyone agrees to the objectives.

Understand the specification

The third milestone requires clarity about the functional and technical requirements for the project. At all stages during the functional and technical requirements definition, the team should be checking back against the business objectives to ensure things are heading in the right direction. Each set of stakeholders should be involved in this review. If it is not possible to understand the functional and technical requirements in sufficient detail to give confidence that you know what you are buying, stop, re-assess and, as necessary, re-do this phase until the confidence level is sufficiently high to enable you to move forward. If you do not understand the requirement, you will not be able to help others understand.

The requirements team needs to understand the business proposition for the procurement—the problem you're trying to solve. If the procurement is simply getting a particular item because you must have that item, then this process may not be appropriate.

Technical requirements should be those that are absolutely necessary for compatibility, performance, or future enhancement. Always question technical requirements that specify a particular supplier's standard or appear arbitrary in terms of specification. Ask why such particular technical requirements are needed. Sometimes a more general way of specifying a technical requirement will be fairer to all suppliers and provide you with a better and more cost-effective solution.

Your company may have particular standards for a system, often industry standard specifications, which many manufacturers meet. Those company standards should be referenced if applicable.

Agree on the acceptance procedure and criteria

It is essential to have a mechanism for determining whether the business requirements, the functional requirements and the technical requirements have all been met.

Acceptance criteria should be aligned and integrated with corporate measures, as well as with prioritization factors. The same criteria used to justify the investment in the first place should be used to measure success. Measures can be qualitative or quantitative. These measures and expectations should be defined upfront and included as baseline performance expectations in the original requirements documentation. Ongoing monitoring will document ongoing improvement and hold the supplier accountable.

Case study: Failure to align objectives leads to contract failure

Executive management at Company A was very clear that they wished to outsource key aspects of their clinical trials procedure to achieve greater flexibility and to encourage innovation. Reduced costs were a potential side-benefit. However, in a procurement process driven by Procurement and Finance, the acceptance criteria became dominated by price, regulatory compliance and supplier acceptance of risk. These measures resulted in elimination of the more creative suppliers and created an environment in which the winning supplier had no incentive to be flexible or creative. In addition, the contract lacked any mechanisms for the on-going communications and forums that would support flexible operations or innovation.

Eighteen months after contract signature, executive management was exasperated by the 'failure' of the supplier to achieve the required objectives. The contract was terminated at significant cost to both parties.

Put in place a robust change management process

Identifying changes requires a clear initial specification. Managing the process means being prepared to hold up the project until the appropriate analysis has been done, and stakeholder sign-off has been obtained. A robust, practical, pragmatic change management process that enables changes to be assessed and approved quickly will contribute greatly to a successful project outcome (see Chapter 17 for a detailed description of the change management process).

 You need to know both why you are buying and what you are buying to know whether your requirement is sufficient to define your purchase and evaluate performance.

7.3 What goes wrong

Requirements often miss the mark. 88 percent of respondents to an IACCM survey indicated that raising the quality of requirements was the number one factor critical to improved contract performance in their organizations.

So what are the issues that arise most commonly in requirements definition?

- They are often incomplete, or lack clarity over relative priorities.
- They may represent someone's view of the solution, rather than reflecting true requirements.
- There is frequently a failure to understand the range of stakeholders who should be included in requirements development, resulting in a flawed requirement.
- There may be ignorance of corporate policies and standards, particularly in companies with multiple divisions or international operations.
- There is a tendency to rush to a solution and specify answers to a problem, rather than describe the need or issue for which a solution or fix is being sought.

Finally, during the lifetime of a deal or relationship, requirements will evolve and conditions will change. To the extent possible, requirements need to take these into account.

 Case study: Fundamental flaws in Australia's new submarine program

Australia's Defence Materiel Organisation (DMO) is responsible for major defense procurements. A recent project involves $9.1 billion, more than one-third of the total defense budget, to acquire 12 new submarines. As Australia's largest-ever defense acquisition, it cannot afford to fail.

Unfortunately, the DMO's previous acquisition of six Australian-built Collins-class submarines was bedevilled with problems. Mechanical failures were so severe that frequently only one of the six submarines was operational. The underlying issue is that Australia does not have a long tradition of submarine building and active construction facilities. The DMO had not understood what was needed for the submarines to operate effectively—adequate infrastructure, access to the necessary industry skills and a properly resourced supply chain.

The new project is twice as ambitious—double the number of home-built submarines, but the endemic failures have not been fixed. Delays in construction and on-going mechanical failures remain almost inevitable. The Australian Senate has concluded that the DMO is repeating the errors that caused cost blowouts, delays and poor performance in the Collins-class submarines and other programs. Their report says: "DMO lacks a robust risk-management regime (and) seems incapable of learning from past mistakes".

However, DMO is perhaps the victim of confused requirements. Decisions to source in the domestic market are generally political in nature (to maintain or build a domestic capability, to provide employment, to develop national skills) and frequently are not compatible with other goals (minimizing cost to the taxpayer, ensuring on-time delivery, avoiding potential reputation risk to the politicians). The real failure in situations like this can sometimes be the unwillingness of executive sponsors to hear the truth, or the reluctance of those overseeing the project to highlight the inconsistencies.

 Improving requirements gathering and analysis is almost guaranteed to improve performance.

7.4 *Constructing an RFI or RFP*

A Request for Information (RFI) and a Request for Proposal (RFP) are very similar. The key difference is that an RFI is used at an earlier stage than an RFP, when the intent to purchase has not yet been established; it is therefore more exploratory in nature and will generally be less precise in specific requirements. An RFI may be issued to facilitate a 'make or buy' decision or it may be issued to gather information to assist business and associated procurement strategy, for instance in an emerging field or in relation to suppliers who are new to the market or from geographies not previously considered.

Different organizations will have different protocols that are followed to develop these documents, which may commonly be referred to as 'RFx' documents. (RFx documents are discussed in more detail in the next chapter.) These RFx documents generally include the following items.

Cover letter

This section of the RFx contains critical information for a successful bid process. It should contain the following minimum information:

- Purpose and objective
- Timeline for response
- Supplier/bidder conference (if one is being held)
- Contact information for buyer
- Dates, times, and mailing address for responses
- Instructions about the change process for changes to the RFx
- Executive overview

The executive overview section of the RFx explains at a very high level what is expected of the supplier's product or service and how it will fit in the overall business process of the customer's organization.

General information

The RFx should inform suppliers if they are required to execute a non-disclosure agreement (NDA). The guidelines for the RFx should describe the process to be used to evaluate each supplier's response and to assess the supplier's relative competitive position with the understanding that the technical requirements outlined in the RFx must be met in order to qualify for consideration.

Other considerations for evaluation will include at a minimum:

- Budgetary costs, including one-time implementation and continuing operations and update costs
- The supplier's Security Plan, ownership information, and details of operations
- Acceptance of key terms and conditions, or the process for variations
- The supplier's financial condition
- The supplier's experience and quality control processes
- Submission of creative approaches/ideas.

Proposal (response) format

It is important that all the suppliers to an RFx understand the format requirements for their responses. These must be consistent in order to allow fair comparison. The suppliers' RFx response format detail should contain:

- A cover letter including the supplier's name, address, and contact information for the person who is authorized to make representations for the supplier.
- Conceptual alternatives and explanations about how they will meet the requirements.
- Feasibility assessment of each proposed alternative.
- Assumptions that the supplier made while preparing the proposal.
- Additional information relative to the RFx; other materials, suggestions, and discussions that are appropriate, etc.
- Any material and data not specifically requested for evaluation, but which the supplier wishes to submit. You may also want the suppliers to include references to those pages that are relevant to the response, such as standard sales brochures, photographs or diagrams and alternative proposals the supplier may want to present.
- Cost and schedule estimates. Depending on the evaluation procedure or company policy these may be presented separately from technical information.

Terms and conditions

Terms and conditions of the RFx need to reflect the specific business circumstances. They should give particular consideration to:

- Confidentiality provisions—these might be very restrictive if the project associated with the RFx is of a highly sensitive nature
- Intellectual property—both to protect the customer's intellectual property and also to address the ability to use content from prospective suppliers' responses in any subsequent RFx
- Specific compliance issues, both regulatory and to any internal policies or practices deemed 'non-negotiable'
- Mapping out the key contractual provisions that are expected to be part of any subsequent contract

Required supplier information

This section contains information relevant to the way the suppliers operate their businesses. It should request detailed technical, financial, quality and management information. This information becomes an important part of the final evaluation process and plays a substantial role in selecting the successful supplier.

Corporate information obtained from the suppliers should include, but not be limited to, financial statements, corporate structure, legal or material restrictions that would preclude the supplier's ability to deliver on a project, any previous work performed for your company or any of your company's subsidiaries, and any similar work done for other organizations relative to the proposed RFx.

 Remember to ask for any information required for a good decision and provide any information necessary for a complete, competitive response.

7.5 Supplier perspective

Requirements are fundamentally important to sellers. When a piece of prospective business is identified, it is critical that the supplier be able to recognize whether that opportunity is one they want to win. In so

doing they prevent valuable time and resources being wasted on opportunities they couldn't win or wouldn't want to win.

A potential contract must be appropriate—that is, it fits within the strengths of the supplier—and commercially sound—that is, it enables the supplier to earn a profit or gain another benefit such as increased market presence or the opportunity of future business. Suppliers need to explore the marketplace by engaging in pre-sales activity to be able to define existing and potential customers, and to create a sales plan (or business plan) based on customer needs and understanding the competition.

This information in the requirement will additionally form a key part of the bid process. With all sales opportunities, time is of the essence. Suppliers need to do what they can to influence a purchaser's decision-making process in their favor as early and as quickly as possible. This improves their chances of success and reduces the opportunities available to their competitors. Timeliness is made more critical with RFIs and RFPs, as they will contain a date by which a response must be submitted. In such situations a supplier bid process is vital to the decision-making process.

Keeping suppliers 'in the dark' prior to RFI and/or insisting on very short timescales limits opportunity for suppliers to fully engage.

Developing a successful response to a customer's request requires that suppliers must understand the context for their product/service and the over-arching business objective being sought. It is not enough to know what a product does. The response must articulate how the product solves the customer's problem. Clearly communicating this information in the requirements allows better decision-making for all parties.

Understanding requirements is the essential first step in a successful project or procurement. These requirements are not limited to technology or functionality—they embody the business objectives for the project, the

needs of all of the stakeholders, and the financial and timescale needs of the organization.

Questions to ask about requirements

☐ *Who are the stakeholders for this project?*

☐ *What does the business want to achieve from this acquisition?*

☐ *Are all of the objectives compatible?*

☐ *Do I understand the functional and technical requirements well enough to explain them to someone else?*

☐ *Do technical specifications include only those items that are necessary for compatibility, performance, or future enhancement?*

☐ *Are company standards met?*

☐ *Are the criteria for accepting the product clear?*

☐ *Is the acceptance procedure explained?*

☐ *How are changes anticipated and handled?*

☐ *As a supplier, is this an opportunity I want to win?*

☐ *Does this fit within the strengths of my company?*

☐ *Can my company make a fair profit and/or gain another benefit?*

7.6 Summary

Effort expended at the beginning of a project to define the requirements and align business and contract strategy yields a much greater chance for a successful project. A better solution, lower costs, and improved implementation and adoption all result from careful and complete requirements definition. Following the guidelines in the chapter will help to ensure that RFx documents contain the necessary information to provide clarity for both buyers and sellers.

CHAPTER 8

BID PHASE: BID AND PROPOSAL MANAGEMENT

It's a very sobering feeling to be up in space and realize that one's safety factor was determined by the lowest bidder on a government contract.

Alan Shepard

This chapter explains the process of managing bids and proposals from a buyer and seller perspective, as well as detailing how objectivity can enhance the process from both perspectives. It also outlines the main RFx documents used by buyers and their impact on sellers.

8.1 *Overview*

The bid process is iterative, where the buyer refines its understanding of the requirement and the potential for the market to meet that requirement, before selecting suitable suppliers, then negotiating and awarding a contract. The process concludes with notifying suppliers of the award decision—both successful and unsuccessful suppliers.

The buyer and seller have complementary perspectives on the bid process, so it is useful to have an insight of what makes an effective bid process from both viewpoints. This section focuses more on sellers than buyers, as the buy-side's formal procurement process is well documented elsewhere.

If the buyer is in the public sector there will be additional rules that they and prospective suppliers must follow, in addition to the normal commercial process. Sellers will need to be aware of the constraints, where relevant, as they will be automatically disqualified from bidding if they do not comply with public sector procurement processes. The rules vary from country to country—different local procedures will apply—but in brief they reflect stricter rules on competition and ethical behavior. There may also be requirements to favor local suppliers, or the converse.

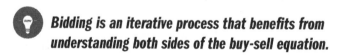 **Bidding is an iterative process that benefits from understanding both sides of the buy-sell equation.**

8.2 *The RFx documents and the buyer perspective*

RFx documents

The buyer needs information to support the purchasing decision. They may request this information from potential suppliers in three different

ways—an RFP / RFI/ or RFQ. The first two letters mean 'Request For' whereas the last letters of 'P', 'Q', and 'I' stand for 'Proposal, 'Quotation or 'Information'. When the three of these are jointly referred to, the term RFx is used (Table 8.1).

Table 8.1   RFx definitions

RFI:	The buyer has little information about the solution and needs to explore an idea or get information from suppliers about how they would solve the buyer's needs.
RFQ:	The buyer has precise information about their proposed purchase (usually a commodity item), there is little variation in the product and they are primarily interested in the best price on the best terms.
RFP:	Used to solicit proposals from suppliers where the buyer has strong and well thought out business requirements.

The RFP takes the most time to prepare and manage. If the buyer can use an RFQ, it will be easier than an RFP. The RFI is usually a preliminary step before issuing an RFP. The RFI helps to gather information to be used in the eventual RFP (or helps the buyer decide not to issue an RFP).

Sometimes a mini-RFP (an RFP with few requirements and few price components) is more appropriate for smaller or less complex procurements.

The RFI/RFQ/RFP may not be appropriate in all cases, especially if time is of the essence or if only one supplier offers the product the buyer wants. This is generally called a sole-source environment. The buyer may want to consider a longer-term commitment with the supplier to lower the price or investigate developing alternative sources of the product or building it/supplying it themselves.

There may be better (and faster) options than using RFQs: electronic business exchanges and reverse auction sites may give faster and lower bids for RFQ-type procurements.

Significant focus was given to developing requirements in the previous chapter. It is assumed that the customer has now determined exactly what problem is to be solved and developed acceptable requirements, ideally in conjunction with potential suppliers. The choice of RFx document reflects the current level of confidence in the requirements. Note that the RFP process is generally only used for a large procurement (whatever your organization considers to be large).

Developing evaluation criteria

An important task when preparing the RFx is to determine how suppliers will be scored and ranked. Objectivity is paramount in this endeavor. The criteria for evaluating the responses at each stage of the RFx must be transparent and fair—otherwise there is the possibility of suppliers challenging the decisions or internal stakeholders feeling their issues have been marginalized. In public procurements, this might lead to a legal challenge.

Managing the supplier—handling questions and making clarifications

The RFx will generally specify the process for communications with the supplier during the bidding process. In many cases it will establish a high level of formality, both with regard to the form that communications can take and with whom the supplier may communicate. If those communications will be shared with other bidders, that must also be specified.

Typical questions that may be received from the suppliers include:

- Clarification on requirements, especially requirements marked as 'must-have'.
- Questions about technical specifications that appear to be linked to a particular vendor.
- Whether there is a confirmed budget for the project.
- Whether management has already internally selected the winning supplier (and that the RFP is just a formality).
- Whether the supplier can propose its own solution, or a variant from the customer specification (one not contemplated by the RFP).

Sometimes questions will bring attention to information in the RFx that is incorrect or incomplete. In these cases all potential suppliers should be notified of the deficiency, provided with the corrected information, and if necessary, have the response date extended to incorporate the changes.

Evaluating responses—overall score

Preparing the overall evaluation can be the most difficult part of the task. Procurements vary too much to give specific guidance on how to combine the requirements score and the cost scores.

Some companies like to use formulas such as ranking the suppliers best to worst on each category, then use a percent factor—for example, requirements score = 45 percent; supplier quality/reputation = 30 percent; cost score = 25 percent—and combine the scores that way. However, simple ordinal rankings ignore percentage differences between the suppliers, so more sophisticated weighting schemes may be desirable.

Some companies employ 'hurdle' functions where suppliers must do better than some satisfactory level on each ranking criterion in order to be considered. For example, a company may have submitted the best requirements answers and have the best (lowest) costs, but have a very bad reputation and be in bankruptcy. Even if their overall score is best, you might use a hurdle function to eliminate them because they received too low a score in an important evaluation category. In public procurements this is often referred to as having a supplier who is both *responsive* to the RFP as well as *responsible* in its management and operations. In order to receive a contract both criteria must be satisfied.

Consider whether you should have a Best and Final Offer (BAFO) bidding round, which provides the suppliers with a solid base from which to make their final offer. This ensures that any requirements that changed during the bidding process are properly addressed and provides the suppliers with the opportunity to provide a more compelling solution. This is more appropriate for large-scale complex requirements.

Conducting a formal evaluation brings objectivity to what may otherwise become an emotional process, with different stakeholders championing favorite suppliers. The discipline of the evaluation process helps to avoid these situations and ensures that the ultimate choice will best serve the business objectives.

A final point to consider is whether the evaluation criteria and weightings will be made known to the suppliers. There are mixed views on this question. The benefit of an open process is that suppliers can adjust their offerings to demonstrate how they would meet those weighted criteria; the disadvantage is that they might distort their claimed capabilities.

Supplier notification and the BAFO process

Generally, it is best practice to have two or three suppliers in the Best and Final Offer bidding round. However, it is easier to manage two suppliers than three (or more) and easier to pick a clear winner.

How many suppliers should be allowed to continue to the BAFO round depends upon the number initially bidding, the competitive nature of the environment, and perhaps some political factors as well as the practicalities of managing a parallel dialogue with two or more suppliers. The decision is also likely to be affected by complexity and cost. Bidding is often an expensive proposition for suppliers and they do not take kindly to being used simply as a way to exert competitive pressure on the final winner.

Proceeding at this time requires reasonable assurances from senior management that resources are available to go forward with a contract award. Failure to make an award after conducting final discussions could seriously damage relationships with key suppliers and lead to accusations of negotiating in bad faith. Unfortunately, lengthy proposal cycles are associated with an RFP and it is not uncommon for business and funding imperatives to change.

The final round is aimed at lowering the cost of the suppliers' proposal and ensuring that the buyer has a good understanding of the solution and the commitment to deliver as specified. Few modifications in requirements, if any, should occur at this point.

BAFO process and final contract

The BAFO suppliers should receive the standard procurement contract or should respond to the standard contract included as an appendix in the RFP.

The suppliers will resist spending time on formally negotiating contract issues in advance of getting the bid; however, leverage is lost unless at

least some negotiation occurs at this time. Some contract terms may be critical to a successful supplier selection and may influence price and cost (warranty and liability, for example). Any representations made by the suppliers in their response to the RFP should be referenced and included in the final contract.

Supplier award notification

The process for choosing the supplier is similar to the one used to select the preliminary suppliers, except criteria may be added that are based on the suppliers' presentations and how the supplier has responded to any new requirements

It is possible that new issues arise at this late stage. They should only be contemplated if failure to do so would invalidate or jeopardize the decision and consequent implementation. The winning supplier(s) should be contacted to finalize any outstanding contractual issues and, once they have been finalized satisfactorily, advised that they have been awarded the contract.

 Checklist: Keys for success

☐ *Preparation: A thorough bid process takes a good deal of preparation and forethought. This yields rewards many times over by having a relatively stress- free procurement.*

☐ *Tailoring: Tailor the size of your RFx efforts to the complexity of the procurement and the associated risks to your company of not having the requirements met.*

☐ *Taking a long-term view: Embark on the RFx process with a view to the end result of a partnership/ relationship with your supplier(s) of choice by treating the prospective suppliers as potential partners rather than future enemies as you go through the bidding process.*

 Choose every step in this process with an awareness of the business problem being solved by the procurement. If all efforts are in line with that, the process will be appropriate to the rewards obtained.

8.3 *Bid and proposal management— the seller perspective*

Bid and Proposal Management may be a centralized organization within the seller's headquarters operations or it may be a team residing within each division or business unit of the company. Some companies assemble a different bid team for each proposal using the expertise of the technical, commercial and financial people closest to the deal.

Many bid teams take the view that 'the contract' can be left until the end of the process. Their motivations for this attitude vary, but it is a mistake that leads either to delay or a badly-structured agreement. A good contract involves intelligent trade-off between the many business factors affecting the deal. Some examples are the technical or functional specifications, the certainty and timing of delivery, costs, price, payment terms, funding options, potential benefits or incremental opportunities and the risks associated with performance shortfalls. These must be evaluated in parallel to ensure that the supplier also takes balanced account of internal requirements and establishes a coherent bid and negotiation strategy embracing all key stakeholders.

Understanding your customer's environment

To adopt a winning bid strategy, the Bid and Proposal group and sales team must develop an in-depth knowledge of the industry and environment in which the customer operates and an understanding of the customer's business issues.

 Understanding the customer, carefully and objectively reviewing the RFx, and combining that information to demonstrate both responsiveness and responsibility increases the chance of getting more work and more profitable work.

External influences

Political influences can be a major factor in the customer's goals and direction. These influences are often discounted because they apply to all companies equally, but they may play a much greater role in some

market sectors such as telecommunications. These considerations include factors such as the current government's direction toward either greater regulation or free market competition.

Economic influences include not just the general economy, but also the specific market economy. The availability of funding for capital expansion and the customer's reliance on external financing are key.

Another important influence in the customer's decision-making is the demographics of their customer base's population and social values. These factors may greatly influence the current and future direction and goals of the customer, especially when they see changes in their own customer base.

Technology is always an issue, sometimes even going beyond the technical requirements of the proposed solution. Understanding the market in which the customer operates is critical, as well as knowing where your current and future systems and solutions will fit and integrate. This is key to writing an effective proposal.

Internal influences
Many of the influences we have touched on so far are external to the customer. In less developed markets, with more government control, these external influences will be primary in establishing the customer's decision factors. In more competitive, free market environments, internal operating and financial influences will be an equivalent or greater factor.

In privately owned corporations, the requirements of satisfying shareholders and generating positive economic numbers and increasing per-share value will be major requirements. How customers internally measure themselves (return on sales, return on assets, return on equity) will be significant factors in procurement decision-making.

In addition to increasing revenue and market share, all companies want to lower their costs of operation. High operating costs may be due to inefficient operating methods, high labor costs, outdated equipment and machinery, effectiveness of sales and distribution channels, or a multitude of other factors. Understanding these internal factors is important in knowing what is critical to the customer and structuring the proposal to highlight the value that you can provide.

As Case Study 2 (in Appendix B) shows, sometimes the customer fails to recognize the value that the supplier adds, especially in a long-term relationship, and blames the supplier for project failure when the real root cause is poor project management as a customer. In this case, the customer became dissatisfied with its supplier of more than 20 years, after a series of projects running over time and budget. They decided that they needed new architecture and new suppliers for an IT contract worth in excess of $1 billion and covering more than 100 countries. What they really needed, however, was commercial ability; their internal teams lacked the skill to coordinate major international projects. Just in time, the supplier realized that this was much more important than technical skills; they beat off their competitors by demonstrating their proven abilities in this area. The key message here is that the customer does not always know what they need, although they usually know what they want—not necessarily the same thing. Successful suppliers know how to focus on meeting that need.

Basing the selling process on customers' buying behavior

All customers go through a series of fairly predictable steps in making a purchase decision in a major sale. It is important to understand how each customer makes its purchasing decisions and to base the team's selling strategies on the customer's specific buying behavior rather than on its own typical steps in the sales process. In most major sales, there are at least a few assumptions that a supplier can make:

- The purchasing decision will be made over a relatively long time period, not in a single meeting or sales call.
- There are competing alternatives (technologies, suppliers) from which the customer will choose.
- There are many risks (to both the customer and supplier) if a bad decision is made.

The phases of the general purchasing decision are outlined below.

1. Recognition of need

During the first phase, the customer begins to be dissatisfied with existing methods, systems, products or suppliers. Competitive pressures, internal cost constraints, political pressures, end-user requirements or the availability of newer technology may trigger this phase. During this phase, buyer dissatisfaction grows until it reaches a critical mass.

 No prior knowledge of the RFI indicates limited chance of success for the supplier.

The buyer will often seek information from prospective sellers by issuing an RFI. This helps them to determine the products and services that are available in the marketplace. It is important at this point that the supplier tries to focus the customer on the broader business issues. Very often, however, a customer may have more than one problem and needs to decide which problem is better solved first. Positioning the company and its particular solutions could influence the customer to solve one problem before the other.

In relationship selling, the sales team would already have a well-developed awareness of the business pressures or other factors influencing the customer's dissatisfaction. The sales team should be viewed by the customer as a consultant who is helping to solve their business problems.

2. Evaluation of options

It is during this period where the supplier company can—and should—have the greatest opportunity to influence the customer's requirements, decision-making criteria and development of the Request for Proposal.

3. Identification of requirements

After a preliminary decision is made to buy a needed system, product or service, the customer must specifically identify its requirements. It must analyze these requirements and be able to describe the desired function, performance and design. Customers who have a trusted relationship with their suppliers may ask them for assistance in determining their requirements, providing that this is allowed under the customer's procurement procedures.

The customer may be evaluating competing technologies, or it may have competing demands on the available budget and need assistance in establishing priorities for investment. Proactive involvement by various members of the sales team, using their understanding of the business environment and commercial options, can have a major influence on the customer's development of specifications. Knowing the key players in this stage and positioning the team experts to influence requirements will pay big dividends.

 Case study: Innovative form of contract leads to success

Facing strong competitive pressures, XYZ Limited needed to reduce costs without damaging the quality of customer service. One initiative focused on how it might reduce warehousing or shipping costs. These were seen as alternatives because tackling both areas simultaneously was considered too risky and too demanding on internal resources. An RFI was issued for both areas to assist internal evaluation.

One of its existing logistics suppliers—NBC Corporation—was aware of the debate within the customer organization and decided to make an innovative proposal. It suggested that there was potential for a consolidated solution based on a shared-benefits contract. NBC Corporation would commit to achieving a minimum level of cost reduction while maintaining or increasing end-customer service levels. It would cover all costs on a 90 day rolling cycle (thereby giving XYZ an immediate cash-flow boost) and then share the overall cost reductions achieved.

This successful proposal could only be made because the sales team at NBC engaged with their commercial experts to devise an innovative form of contract, which required thorough financial and procedural evaluation to ensure viability. It resulted in NBC growing the value of their existing contract by more than 400% and eliminating competitors from the account.

4. Establishing decision criteria

Once the customer has determined the requirements, they need to establish the decision criteria by which they will evaluate competing sources for meeting the requirements.

 It is essential to ensure all suppliers have all appropriate information on an equitable basis.

It is at this point that customers are generally open to multiple supplier presentations and are trying to narrow the field of competitors to those considered fully qualified to fulfill the needs. Customers will generally use pre -established criteria to screen potential suppliers and then to make the final selection. During this phase, the sales team should have three goals:

- Uncover decision criteria—to find out which factors or criteria the customer intends to use to make choices between suppliers. Will price be more important than quality? Will delivery schedule be an influencing factor? Reliability? After sale service? Compatibility with existing equipment?
- Influence decision criteria—to try to introduce criteria or factors which should be important in making the decision but which the customer may not have considered. Also to influence the relative importance of the customer's existing criteria so that your offer will be judged favorably against competitors.
- Maximize perceived fit with decision criteria—to demonstrate to the customer that your offer adequately fits those criteria that will be used to make the decision.

As a supplier, the more you can influence the customer's decision criteria to match your strengths and minimize your weaknesses, the greater the chances of getting the work, and a greater likelihood of it being profitable work.

Attempts to influence the customer's buying behavior and decision criteria should always be part of the strategy and relationship planning for the account. One reason that 'the contract' is often seen as a problem is because attempts to influence the customer's position on terms and conditions is left too late. Educating customers on issues such as payment terms, performance criteria or risk allocation is an on-going process in which the sales or project team will most likely need the active participation of contract, finance or legal experts. Waiting until the heat of the bid or negotiation is generally far too late.

Checklist: Bid and proposal questions to ask

For the buyer:

☐ *Which type of procurement is best suited for my acquisition?*

☐ *What evaluation criteria are important?*

☐ *Can the business goals be achieved with buying standard products and discriminating only on price?*

☐ *Is my solicitation complete—asking all questions I need to have answered and providing suppliers with sufficient information?*

☐ *Have I specified communication channels?*

☐ *Do I really need a BAFO?*

For the seller:

☐ *What are the external influences of my customer?*

☐ *What are their internal influences?*

☐ *Do I understand their buying behavior?*

☐ *What are the evaluation criteria?*

☐ *How can I best influence the decision making process?*

☐ *What are the competing technologies for this acquisition?*

☐ *What are the risks/consequences to my customer and me for failure?*

8.4 Summary

The bid process is often iterative, and both buyer and seller should be prepared for a lengthy process. With that being said, the more efficient the process is, the lower the cost for both the buyer and seller. The cost to purchase anything should be commensurate with its value and importance to the company strategy.

The evaluation of proposals is highly individualized, with some acquisitions based solely on price and others based heavily on technical

competence. Any evaluation should consider the elements of responsiveness and responsibility.

Involvement of appropriate specialists from finance, legal, and commercial organizations at the bid phase can shorten the time required in later stages as expectations are established early. Education of both buyers and sellers during the bid process is fundamental.

The greatest opportunity for a profitable project comes when the technical strengths of a seller are matched to genuine buyer needs.

 Understanding the customer, carefully and objectively reviewing the RFx, and combining that information to demonstrate both responsiveness and responsibility increases the chance of getting more work and more profitable work.

CHAPTER 9

DEVELOP PHASE: SELECTING A CONTRACT TYPE

Begin with the end in mind.

Stephen Covey

The Develop phase should ideally begin with a simple question: **What business needs to be done?** The answer to that question should guide the selection of the proper contract type at the beginning of the task and will ultimately add speed to the entire commercial transaction process.

Business relationships take many forms, so contracts take many forms. Choosing the right agreement at the beginning saves countless hours during the remainder of the process because the proper terms, and only the proper terms, are negotiated. There is no need to draft and negotiate terms involving intellectual property for the sale of commercial machinery!

The word 'contract' usually describes only a particular type of formal agreement, but the critical factor is not the type of writing, or whether writing exists at all, but the extent and intent of a party's promise.

This chapter provides a brief overview of the following five chapters (Chapter 10 through Chapter 14), which describe the major types of business relationships and the issues arising in each.

9.1 *Preliminary agreements*

The early stages of a commercial relationship can vary greatly, from informal conversations and exploration through to some kind of documented initial understanding. The key considerations are the extent to which the parties are making a binding commitment and the need for commercial confidentiality.

Non-disclosure agreements are often entered into, to protect sensitive commercial information. The main points to agree are whether there are mutual obligations, clarity about what is confidential and the period of protection for commercially sensitive information.

A **Memorandum of Understanding** and/or **Letter of Intent** can be useful, to document the preliminary understanding of the intent of the commercial arrangement. Their main purpose should be to simply identify and document the key business and contractual issues that will form the basis of a formal contract. However, these can be extremely risky because of the likelihood of introducing unintended liabilities; they must be used with caution.

9.2 Selling goods and services

Sale of goods only is a simple form of contract: its main elements are a clear description of what is being purchased, its price, and delivery terms.

Contracts for services vary in complexity, depending on the nature of the service and how critical it is to the business. A service contract covers agreed descriptions of its scope, the timeline for performance, charges and payment, liability, intellectual property (where applicable) and arrangements for termination of the contract.

Contracts for the combined sale of goods (products) and services define both the goods and the specific services associated with the goods. They have to address the unique terms for both products and services: price and payment, warranties (guarantees), and liability.

9.3 Licenses and leases

Licenses and leases are similar to contracts for sale. **Licenses** are usually related to software, with key elements such as terms of use. **Leases** are usually related to real property (tenancies) or financing arrangements for capital expenditure.

9.4 Other business relationships

Some contracts are solely about commercial relationships. A party may sell 'through' another party, as an **agent or distributor**, which is often the only way to do business in a particular market. There are significant global variations in laws about these kinds of relationship.

Alternatively, parties may agree to sell 'with' each other, through **business consortia, joint ventures or alliances**. In these situations the key issues include legal liability for the party's own company and the extent to which the party is responsible for the performance of other parties.

9.5 *Complex and specialized agreements*

It may be necessary to enter into a different type of arrangement because of the complexity of integrating a number of services—this is common in major construction or IT projects.

Outsourcing is another area where specialized agreements may be required; for example, a major bank may be outsourcing some aspects of its business and has to consider areas such as security and disaster recovery across a global network.

CHAPTER 10

DEVELOP PHASE: PRELIMINARY AGREEMENTS

The game is afoot!

Sir Arthur Conan Doyle

The early stages of a commercial relationship vary greatly. In some cases the beginnings may be very structured and formal, as in a bidding process with a public entity. Other situations may be more informal, for example interactions such as trade show meetings or introductions by mutual associates. Regardless of the circumstances, at some point it becomes necessary to document and structure the relationship.

The first phase of this relationship building is often the protection of confidential information that is shared, which is sometimes followed by a documentation of other issues. This chapter will look at some of these agreements in more detail.

10.1 *Non-disclosure agreements*

A non-disclosure agreement (NDA), as outlined previously, is simply a contract in which the parties promise to protect the confidentiality of certain information that is disclosed during a business transaction. These may also be known as confidentiality agreements. NDAs are frequently included as part of the employer-employee relationship and may also incorporate provisions prohibiting future competition. This section does not deal with these specific issues; it focuses exclusively on the commercial transaction process.

During initial contacts, where only general ideas are being discussed, there is usually no particular legal relationship between the parties. As the discussions continue obligations can be placed upon one or both of the parties. A non-disclosure agreement is often introduced to cover exploratory talks as they become more specific.

 Both parties should make it clear whether they do or do not wish to incur obligations on behalf of themselves or the other party at this point in time.

Questions often arise as to the point where a confidentiality agreement is necessary. Simply asking the question, "If this information was given to a competitor would it be damaging?" is often the most useful

barometer. If the answer to that question is "Yes", a non-disclosure agreement should be put in place.

However, if the discussions are related to any sort of invention or new idea, it is wise to immediately seek advice, whether you are the owner or the recipient of the information.

Non-disclosure agreements are typically classified as either 'one-way' (unilateral) or mutual. A unilateral agreement is used when only one party will be disclosing information. A mutual non-disclosure is used when both parties will be receiving and disclosing confidential information.

 Case study: "There are no secrets"

Competitive pressure was forcing a large computer manufacturer (Company X) to become more flexible in its customer negotiations. It decided to respond through a 'special bid' process that resulted in terms and conditions that were tailored for each customer. However, the Finance department and Sales management were nervous about these terms becoming known on the wider market, so they required each customer to sign a non-disclosure agreement.

Some time later, a manager from Company X attended a conference at which many of its customers were present. He was surprised when one of those customers, as part of his presentation, asked the audience: "How many of you have entered into a special deal with Company X?" About 20 hands shot up and participants then started to share the terms of the special agreements they had signed.

Not surprisingly, when the manager reported this to the Company X lawyers, no action was taken.

In most cases, both RFIs and RFPs contain information that is commercially sensitive to the purchaser. In some cultures, the purchaser will wish to protect such information by requiring all intended recipients to sign a non-disclosure agreement before issuing the RFI or RFP. From the supplier's perspective, the information provided in response will also be commercially sensitive in that it will detail some or all of the following areas:

- Current strategy and possibly future direction
- Current and possibly future technology
- Service capabilities
- Operational methodology
- Pricing
- Existing customers or market potential

In this situation it is important to both parties to have an NDA in place before sensitive information is released.

Like other contracts, the NDA should be simple and straightforward, containing only the terms that are necessary for the exchange of commercially confidential information. Five specific areas should be covered in the document:

- Definition of confidential information
- Exclusions from confidential information
- Obligations of the parties
- Time period
- Miscellaneous provisions

Definition of confidential information

The parties must know and agree what information is considered confidential. A broad, over-reaching statement that "everything is confidential" does not speed up the process or provide any real protection. By default, if everything is confidential then potentially nothing is confidential. The document must provide a means for everyone to know what is to be protected. While this is a challenging task, the objective is to describe the information in enough detail to be specific, but without actually disclosing the information. Defining broad categories of information such as customer lists, financial information, marketing plans, or software generally accomplishes this.

Some agreements also contain the requirement for confidential information to be marked with a designation such as 'proprietary' or 'confidential' to be protected. The benefits of doing this are that it can focus the mind to assess what is truly confidential and ensures clarity about what should be protected. The dangers are that people either

forget to mark documents appropriately or simply mark everything, which dilutes the impact of such marking in practice.

Exclusions from confidential information

There are numerous exceptions to the requirement for confidentiality. The following types of information cannot generally be protected by a non-disclosure agreement:

- Information already in the public domain
- Information that becomes public through no fault of the recipient
- Information that is independently developed without reliance on the disclosure

 Case study: The danger of misclassification

A large technology company (Company A) was approached by a much smaller organization (Company B) that had been developing new biometric software. Anticipating that this software could be of considerable value, a business unit manager at Company A entered into an NDA so that she could share a range of confidential data, including some of their own market development plans. After lengthy review, the software was found to have fundamental flaws and discussions were terminated. However, unknown to the business unit manager, another division of Company A had been developing similar software. When this was announced to the market, Company B accused Company A of stealing its intellectual property and cited the terms of the NDA. A substantial out-of-court settlement was agreed.

In this case, it had been a fundamental error to enter into the standard NDA. The business unit manager should have been clear that exchanges related to the new software were not confidential.

Obligations of the parties

Non-disclosure agreements put an obligation on the recipient to hold and keep the proprietary information in confidence and to limit its use. Different agreements may specify different obligations, but it is often expressed as a requirement for the recipient to use the same standard of care to protect confidential information it receives as it uses to protect its own confidential data. Typically the receiving party cannot breach the confidential relationship or induce others to breach it.

Time period
Two time periods are important in a non-disclosure agreement.

The first time period is the time during which disclosures are made. If the NDA is part of the proposal process or is designed to cover exploratory talks about future business the time period may be relatively short. If the NDA is to govern an extended course of dealings it would likely be for a longer period because the business relationship is different.

The second time period is the length of time for which the confidentiality obligations survive. The time period is generally stated as a period of years from either the date of last disclosure or the date the agreement is signed. This time period varies by geographic region. In the US many companies use a five-year standard, although there is some movement toward two- and three-year terms. In Europe it is not unusual to have ten-year terms.

It is common for non-disclosure agreements to be incorporated into software licenses. In these cases confidentiality obligations may be for an indefinite timeframe and end only if specified conditions are met such as

- Information was known or becomes known to the receiving party without obligation of confidentiality.
- Information is independently developed by the receiving party.
- Disclosure is required by law or a governmental agency.

A prime consideration to determine the reasonableness of a term is to look at the information being disclosed. If it is intellectual property that is not likely to go into the public domain such as software or inventions, a longer term is appropriate. If the information is a marketing plan that will be executed over the next twelve months a shorter term meets the business need.

Miscellaneous provisions
Non-disclosures, like most agreements, contain other standard clauses that are considered to be part of a company's 'boilerplate'. This would

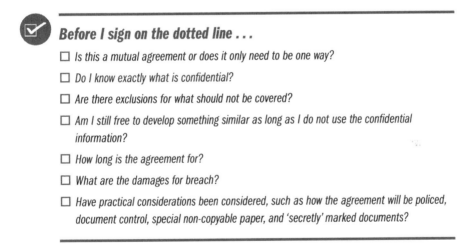

include things such as how disputes will be resolved, which law will govern the document, and (probably most significantly for an NDA) an acknowledgement of damages if the agreement is breached. Most agreements contain a provision to allow the discloser to obtain a court order to stop the release of its information. This is called an injunction or obtaining injunctive relief.

Non-disclosure agreements serve an essential purpose. They allow businesses to proceed with discussions of commercially sensitive matters without fear that future business will be harmed by the discussions.

 Both parties benefit by a mutual non-disclosure agreement. The hardest—and riskiest—part of such agreements is to ensure proper recording and safeguarding of information.

Before I sign on the dotted line . . .

- ☐ Is this a mutual agreement or does it only need to be one way?
- ☐ Do I know exactly what is confidential?
- ☐ Are there exclusions for what should not be covered?
- ☐ Am I still free to develop something similar as long as I do not use the confidential information?
- ☐ How long is the agreement for?
- ☐ What are the damages for breach?
- ☐ Have practical considerations been considered, such as how the agreement will be policed, document control, special non-copyable paper, and 'secretly' marked documents?

10.2 *Memorandum of Understanding*

A Memorandum of Understanding (MoU) is often used to record the progress of a negotiation. Its purpose may be to establish and formalize the baseline of agreements already reached, or is sometimes for the benefit of a third party—for example a financing institution—to demonstrate the extent of progress and confirm authenticity.

However, the MoU may be essentially the same as a Letter of Intent (described below) and similar considerations should be applied to its development and use.

10.3 *Letters of Intent*

The Letter of Intent can provide a vital bridge to help a business professional to move from discussions to a final contract. This type of document is not, however, without its limitations. Its main purpose should be to simply identify and document the key business and contractual issues that will form the basis of a formal contract.

In a business environment obsessed with speed, where customers and sales professionals have contracts they assert must be completed almost instantaneously, the Letter of Intent has become a popular 'convenience' measure and has extended beyond its original intended scope. These types of preliminary agreements do have a place in business, but only under very controlled circumstances. A great deal of obligation and liability can arise with their use.

A binding contract or not?

Letters of Intent are frequently intended to be non-binding, but because they contain all the elements of a contract they may prove binding on the parties. If the parties do not intend the Letter of Intent to be binding, it must be explicitly stated. If the Letter of Intent stays silent on whether it is non-binding, then it is presumed to be binding and enforceable in the courts. Other conflicts in language may also be interpreted to make the document binding, so extreme caution must be used to draft the agreement.

If the document authorizes either of the parties to take some action (e.g. order materials and supplies, obtain government approvals), it is more likely to be considered binding.

The concept of pre-contractual liability is common in civil law countries (we explain the differences between civil law and common law earlier in the book). It provides for a recovery of damages against the party whose conduct prevents the formation of a final contract.

Brevity is a virtue

A Letter of Intent is one place where too much specificity can harm the business. As a general rule, brevity is recommended, and it is better to include just enough details to get the parties started. The more detail about price, work and performance terms, the more likely it will be held to be an enforceable contract.

Dangers

Usually, the business needs to have 'something to get started', or something the customer can use to get financing. The customer will say that all they need is a temporary Letter of Intent that "doesn't really mean anything", and that the parties can replace the letter of intent with a 'real' contract later. Thinking the Letter of Intent is not really binding, customers will often make over-broad statements of the seller's commitments. These statements, in written form with the signatures of the parties, form a contract that can be enforced against the seller, and it probably will be if the seller decides not to continue with the transaction. The Letter of Intent may commit the seller to perform and the buyer to pay, but it may not be sufficient for the seller to recognize the revenue from the sale on its account books. This has a disastrous affect on profitability because there are substantial expenses incurred but no offsetting revenue.

While the first danger of a Letter of Intent is the promises it contains, the second danger is what it does not contain. Usually, other than the statements about what the parties will do and some vague language about the parties negotiating "in good faith", the Letter of Intent contains no terms and conditions. Thus, all other disputed issues will be left up to the law, which will generally mean a negative impact upon one or both parties.

The third danger is that once the customer has the seller's written commitment on a piece of paper, the customer has no incentive (and the seller has no leverage) to negotiate a contract that protects them.

Another danger is that once the Letter of Intent is completed and work begins, both parties will 'forget' to negotiate a final contract and will leave the Letter of Intent as the only document governing the transaction.

The final danger is one that goes toward the heart of negotiation. It is often tempting to defer the discussion of difficult issues until final contract negotiation. This may prove shortsighted and lead to an inefficient use of resources. It is often better to address tough issues early in the process. If there is an issue that is a 'deal killer', it is advantageous to recognize this early, disengage, and redeploy the resources to another opportunity

The best options

The best alternative is not to create a Letter of Intent in the first place, but instead to speedily develop a contract that contains all the elements and protections that both parties need. This channels the drive for speed in a positive direction rather than allowing it to become an excuse for carelessness.

In situations where a Letter of Intent is truly necessary, it should be drafted to reflect no more commitment than intended, should contain a limit of expenditure, should include or incorporate by reference both parties' standard terms and conditions, and should contain a clear 'drop-dead' date, at which time unless replaced by a contract, the Letter of Intent will expire. It should also include a clear understanding of what will happen if the objective of the Letter of Intent is not achieved.

In pre-contractual negotiations, both parties must be aware of and consider each other's legitimate interests. As negotiations progress, this obligation increases. Each party in the pre-contractual phase should bear its own costs and risks and should not assume obligations or liability toward the other party in the event that negotiations are discontinued. In the event of careless or negligent dealing, problems are likely to occur.

 __The Letter of Intent is probably the most dangerous written form that a contract can take.__

 ### Before I sign on the dotted line . . .

☐ *Does the Letter of Intent clearly state whether it is binding or non-binding?*

☐ *What exactly is required of both parties?*

☐ Does it contain a limit of expenditure?

☐ Does it contain the necessary 'boilerplate' clauses to provide the protections of a contract?

☐ Is there a clear expiration date by which the Letter of Intent is to be replaced by a contract?

☐ What is the impact if the Letter of Intent is not followed by a contract?

10.4 Summary

Contracts are often useful in the early stages of a business relationship. They can define the roles and responsibilities and clarify the expectations of the parties. All business relationships carry an element of risk, and preliminary agreements are effective tools to manage that risk. However, Letters of Intent should be avoided if possible, as they can introduce new risks.

Confidentiality can be a major factor in ongoing relationships, so non-disclosure agreements should not be neglected as a deal moves through the transaction process.

CHAPTER 11

DEVELOP PHASE: SELLING GOODS AND SERVICES

Risk comes from not knowing what you're doing.

Warren Buffett

The actual 'selling' is the part of the commercial transaction process that generally receives the most attention. This focus does not guarantee clarity, but it is important to note that clarity is essential for a successful project. The parties need to be absolutely clear as to the intent of the contract and the specific meaning of the individual clauses.

Contracts provide considerable flexibility for the parties to agree to terms that suit the specific transaction. Differences in the goods and services being bought and sold determine the terms of any contract to a great extent. However, it is important to understand that there may be other terms that are included in the contract by virtue of the type of contract or the location of delivery/performance.

11.1 Sale of goods only

Contracts for the sale of tangible goods are generally considered the simplest type of contract because they do not deal with the complexities of services or the integration of products and services. The most significant element in a contract for the sale of goods is a clear description of what is being purchased, its price, and delivery terms.

The product

The contract must clearly state what is being bought or sold. This may sound simple, but in practice it becomes much more difficult. When shopping in a retail environment for goods, the purchaser is able to make many product decisions almost unconsciously. Using a contract means that those product decisions are deliberate and documented to the extent that anyone can see if the contract has been fulfilled.

The first element of product definition should be a **general description** of the type of item being sold. Making a related example to the snow-shoveling scenario, think about the purchase of a snow-shovel. One of the first considerations would be size. Is it a small shovel to be folded and carried in a car, a medium size that is lightweight, or a large shovel to clear the maximum area? Is it red or blue? Are there any unique characteristics? Is the scraper smooth edged or serrated? Is a particular brand important?

Quality is the second focus. If no quality is specified it is assumed that the goods will be fit for their ordinary purpose. For a snow-shovel this might entail specifying the weight of snow to be lifted or the material from which the shovel is made. It is important to note if warranties are provided or if the goods are sold 'as is' with no expressed or implied warranties.

The final component of the product description is **quantity**. It should specify not only the number being ordered but also the unit of measure. One can refer to a single snow-shovel, a single case, a gross, or just about any other quantity.

Product checklist

☐ Is there a clear description of the type of goods?

☐ Are specifications contained in an RFP or RFI included?

☐ Is there a particular brand important?

☐ How is quality denoted?

☐ Is there a warranty or are goods sold 'as is?'

☐ If there is a warranty, what is the length and is it repair, replace or refund?

☐ How many are being purchased?

☐ Is the unit of measure clear?

The price

The price is generally expressed both as a total price and as a price per unit of measure. This unit of measure is most often tied to the quantity in the product description. The pricing information should also include any other costs and whether (or not) they are included in the total price previously stated. This would include items such as delivery charges, duties, warranties, and taxes. If the price is subject to adjustment, based on circumstances such as the cost of raw materials or fuel or validity until a certain date, this point should be clearly noted.

Any price discounts should also be specified, especially if these are contingent in any way. For example, a discount may depend on a minimum quantity being accepted or might apply if payment is received within a specified timeframe. Ensure there is no ambiguity or error related to the discount; for example, one invoice mistakenly stated that the price to an academic institution was 25% of the retail price, when it should have stated 25% off the retail price.

Payment terms and any payment assurances are also critical. For international transactions, currency and rate of exchange should be stated. Particular care is necessary when an international transaction involves two countries whose currency has the same name. A US supplier lost a significant amount of money by simply pricing in 'dollars'; this resulted in the supplier being paid in New Zealand Dollars rather than the expected US Dollars.

Price checklist

☐ Is the price stated as a specified total price or a price given per unit (or by weight or other measurement)?

☐ Is there any adjustment to prices based on circumstances? If so, is this explained?

☐ Is the treatment of any other costs detailed, such as delivery charges, taxes and duties?

☐ Are the method and terms of payment and invoicing stated?

☐ Is there a specific reference to the currency and/or exchange rate to be used, where applicable?

Delivery terms

Delivery terms must be clear and suit the business purpose. The terms should provide for a specific shipping or delivery date or a means to determine the date. The responsibility for the goods in transit should be stated. This is frequently stated as the transfer of title to the goods. If acceptance occurs at delivery this should be noted. The definitions provided by ICC's Incoterms are a very useful tool to ensure clarity.

There are some key issues and differences related to delivery that must be understood. For example, in the United States, title typically transfers on shipment (itself a term that has limited use elsewhere). This is because the supplier retains a right of repossession until payment is made. However, in many other countries, title does not pass until payment is received. Similar thought must be given to topics such as insurance liability and risk of loss.

Delivery and acceptance are also interconnected terms. In many cases, customers require the right to inspect goods either prior to, or on, delivery. They may even retain a right of rejection for some period of time after they are first put into use. Such terms have significant impact on costs and risks, including whether or not the revenue from the contract can be formally recognized in the seller's accounts.

Delivery terms may allow for delays related to circumstances beyond either party's control, or for other specified circumstances. For delay within the supplier's control, the contract should address whether there are consequences (e.g. penalties) for such delays. Business objectives, and whether alternative sources of supply exist, will determine if a penalty is warranted; this will incentivize the supplier to minimize the possibilities of delays.

Delivery checklist

☐ Do delivery and acceptance occur together? If not, what are the arrangements for acceptance?

☐ Do the delivery terms state a specific shipping date or a means of determining the date?

☐ Is there any allowance for delays related to circumstances beyond either party's control, or for other reason? If so, is this specified clearly?

☐ When and where does the title of ownership transfer from the seller to the buyer?

These fundamentals may seem so basic as not to need any discussion. However, in actual performance it is very common for parties to fail to clearly state these essential requirements. In a recent IACCM survey over 85 percent of respondents rated improved requirements definition as critical for improving their performance.

Before I sign on the dotted line . . .

☐ Do I know exactly what is being bought, and is it specified in clear, unambiguous terms?

☐ Is there a warranty or other assurance of quality?

☐ *What is the price, both per item and total?*

☐ *Does the price include taxes, delivery and duties?*

☐ *How do I accept the product?*

☐ *What is the delivery date?*

11.2 **Contracts for services**

Service contracts range from trash removal to technology consulting services. As with other contracts, the type of service being bought or sold determines much of the detail in the agreement. This section will first deal with general terms of service contracts and then explore some essentials for a Statement of Work (SOW).

Scope of services

The functional and technical requirements need to address the business objective or purpose. The scope of services should state the desired output or outcome, but not necessarily how it is to be achieved. This statement of requirements will vary depending on the service involved. In the snow-shoveling example, a contract might have stated that the walkway was to be clear of snow and ice.

Timeline for performance

If a time-based schedule is required for service delivery, it should be developed before beginning the project. The schedule should identify each task and deliverable, from beginning to end of the project. Experts familiar with the service should validate this schedule so it is not simply a guess. This provides a base timeline, which may be used for performance measurement.

Some contracts do not require a timeline to be developed. These would include services that are performed on a recurring basis such as weekly or monthly, as well as those that are performed only when there is a triggering event, such as a snowfall.

Charges and payment

The services contract must specify how the charges will be calculated. If the service is extremely well defined or repetitive in nature the pricing

may be fixed for the deliverable. Examples of this would include a fixed rate for weekly trash removal or a fixed cost for setting up a new computer and installing a suite of software products for a business.

In situations where the scope is not well defined or the level of effort may vary, hourly rates are generally specified. These may also fall within a range based on individual expertise, licenses, or certifications. Examples of this include engineering services where a licensed professional engineer bills at a higher rate than an engineer or where a qualified plumber would bill more than an apprentice.

Contracts may specify both methods, particularly in the case of a large agreement covering multiple types of service. In this case there must be a clear distinction between the services that are included in the fixed price and those that are billed on an hourly basis. A process for adding fixed price elements may also be included.

For extended term contracts any allowed rate changes should be specified—for example, annual increase in rates in line with agreed indices. Frequently pricing caps are included that limit the price escalation to a certain percentage. It is important to remember the purpose of negotiating a price cap. A buyer wants to exercise some certainty and control over rising costs, but an unreasonable escalation factor may cause a vendor to eventually deploy less experienced labor. This could cause a disruption in service quality.

Payment terms vary as much as the services they cover. Hourly service contracts may be billed monthly on the basis of hours expended. Fixed costs may be billed on a recurring basis for the number of times the service was performed.

'Milestone billing' is a concept that is found mainly in services contracts. For contracts where the final deliverable is something that may be developed over a period of time, it is not uncommon for payment to be tied to the completion of certain milestones. If an end-product is an environmental assessment report, for example, the payment terms may be 60 percent upon completion of the first draft, 25 percent upon completion of any revisions, and the final payment upon acceptance of a final report.

As explained in the description related to the sale of goods, acceptance is not a unique requirement of services contracts. However, because service contracts generally define relationships, there is sometimes a question as to the acceptability of a deliverable. Many contracts specify that services are rendered and deemed accepted at the time performed. Others, especially those tied to milestones, may allow some verification by the buyer that the work meets predetermined quality standards.

If an acceptance test or period is defined in the contract the criteria should be explicit. These agreed-to criteria should detail both parties' obligations relative to the performance of the deliverables. Suppliers will want the acceptance period to be brief so that payment is not withheld for an extended period.

The criteria must be objective measuring tools so both parties will know when a deliverable is acceptable and complete. Once the supplier specifies that a deliverable is complete, acceptance testing should begin. The deliverable will be accepted or rejected according to predefined (and mutually approved) procedures and criteria detailed in the contract.

The practice of withholding a portion of a payment, often called retention, is frequently used in services contracts, though is again not unique to services. In this case, one vendor may be providing services that will be integrated with other vendors. The retention may be used as a performance incentive or to encourage cooperation. The supplier, however, may require full or substantial payment in the event that the customer uses the deliverables or derives other benefit before granting acceptance. There is a risk for either the supplier or the customer to use the payment terms to extract concessions from the other party. For example, a supplier knows that the customer needs to put their solution into operation and uses that as a pressure point to avoid fixing faults; or a customer uses the supplier's almost defect-free product and limits the supplier's access to resolve the remaining defects. It is, therefore, essential that there is clarity about any amounts that may be retained and how such retention may be released.

Liability

Buyers and sellers have different views on liability, and striking a balance can be a challenge. This is indicated by the fact that the liability

and indemnity provisions consistently top the IACCM chart of the most frequently negotiated terms and conditions.

Suppliers take a view that risks should be shared, whereas the buyer would prefer to allocate as much risk as possible onto the supplier. Each has legitimate concerns that need to be balanced with the degree of caution each should reasonably take. For example, sellers should be obligated not to misrepresent the capabilities of their service; it is reasonable to expect they should be penalized for dishonesty, lack of integrity or lack of care in understanding the buyer's needs. Similarly, there should be disincentives to non-performance—for example, if a better offer comes along or if it simply isn't convenient to continue meeting their obligations.

On the other hand, the buyer also has some responsibility in this: they must analyze and describe their requirements sufficiently to enable a reasonable assessment of service suitability. They must also be honest and realistic about their business capabilities to absorb or handle the product or service. And they must recognize that if they wish to hold the supplier absolutely to their commitments, it is only reasonable for a similar expectation from the other side—and similar consequences if they fail.

One major issue here is the level of impact—for either side—if the deal goes wrong or if performance does not meet the expected quality standards. The consequences—and hence the risks—vary dramatically and are not necessarily directly related to the cost of the product or service. For example, failure could significantly impact market reputation; or it might have consequential impacts on another large contract; or it could result in high-profile regulatory breach.

Sellers performing services will wish to accept liability only for actions under their direct control; as a general principle, the liability should be limited to direct damages, no greater than the amount the buyer has paid for the performance of the contract. There are, however, certain instances where a supplier should accept greater exposure to risk where their failure to perform exposes the customer in areas such as confidentiality or data protection. These situations need to be carefully considered and managed, with insurance cover being an option for consideration. There are also areas where they cannot limit liability—for example, in the event of death or injuries due to negligence.

Liability and indemnity terms are made more complex by the extent of international variation. They tend to be in an area where public policy intervenes, but even when left to the courts the frequency of litigation on these topics leads to continuous evolution of the clause, its expression and interpretation. This is why most businesses insist on the involvement of qualified attorneys in drafting and reviewing these clauses.

The buyer may want to recover other forms of (consequential) loss and may want 'per incident' compensation. It is important to consider the likelihood of an event occurring and the scale of its impacts.

There is also a consequential risk if the contract is too punitive or seeks a high limit of liability. In this situation it is likely that the supplier will not attempt any innovation that could ultimately be of benefit to the customer for fear of a failure, which could have serious financial consequence on the supplier.

Suppliers will generally insist on exclusions from liability if any losses are due to the provision of false, misleading or incomplete information or documentation or the acts or omissions of any person other than the supplier.

It is important to remember that nothing in the contract is permitted to have the effect of restricting the supplier's liability in respect of any kind of loss, damage or liability that cannot or must not be excluded or limited under law.

As a final point, many negotiations become entrenched in lengthy debate over liabilities and risk allocation. This is often because the business people have failed to take steps that might have facilitated more intelligent discussion. First, they tend to avoid these clauses (which is understandable), but as a result they leave them until the very end, when there is nothing else to negotiate. This makes an adversarial compromise almost inevitable, so it is wise to involve the lawyers early. Second, many business people fail to think about ways that they might reduce risk probability (which would make these issues of consequence somewhat less important). iI is important that those forming the contract understand and address the factors that are most likely to generate failure.

Before I sign on the dotted line . . .

☐ Have the risks been properly identified?

☐ Are there appropriate management processes in places to manage risk?

☐ Have the parties considered who is best placed to manage the specific risk associated with the contract?

☐ Does the contract reflect that consideration?

☐ Has the cultural impact of the contract been considered? Will there be a blame culture or a success culture?

Intellectual property

Intellectual property is a creation of the mind, such as literature, a design, a piece of art, software, or an invention. It is granted special legal protection depending upon the type of work that it is. Common types of intellectual property rights include copyright, trademarks, patents, industrial design rights and in some jurisdictions trade secrets.

- **Patents** protect inventions and generally last for 20 years
- **Copyright** protects works of authorship that are in a tangible form such as books, music, and artwork. The protection generally lasts for 50 years beyond the life of the author. It is denoted by the symbol ©, although this may not be a legal requirement. (In the UK, Design Rights are similar to copyright and may be registered or unregistered. However, the period of protection for an unregistered design is only 15 years).
- **Trademarks** protect words, names, symbols, sounds, or colors that distinguish goods and services. Trademarks, unlike patents, can be renewed forever as long as they are being used in business. A trademark is denoted by the symbol ®
- **Trade secrets** are information that companies keep secret to give them an advantage over their competitors. The formula for *Coca-Cola* is the most famous trade secret.

The creator generally owns the intellectual property and then grants a license for others to use the product. A services contract that specifies a deliverable that would be granted some type of legal protection should specify the ownership. If ownership is not specified, it remains with the creator.

The issue of ownership of the intellectual property rights in a work product is critical and frequently contentious in a services contract. The customer will often demand ownership, typically by defining the output as 'work made for hire'. In some cases, this is a legitimate requirement—for example, where the customer has provided the design or original ideas. In others, there may be a legitimate concern, such as maintaining competitive advantage or protecting confidentiality—or even over continued right of use (for example, of a consulting methodology or a training program). The supplier will need to decide on a commercial basis whether the customer should own or share the intellectual property rights in the work product.

 Case study: Patents as a destructive weapon

In any contract involving software it is essential to check that suppliers have appropriate ownerships, trading rights, licenses and so on. Failure to do so can be very costly, because the big companies use patents in a predatory way, not as an aid to innovation.

In 2011, Apple and Google spent more on patent lawsuits and patent purchases than they did on research and development of new products. Between 2009 and 2011, in the smartphone industry alone, some $20 billion has been spent on patent litigation and patent purchases. For major companies today, patents are not about innovation; they are about competitive weapons.

The patent system seems to work for most industries, but in the technology sector it has resulted in endless high-profile litigation and threats that frequently put small and innovative companies out of business. The problem is that patents on software often effectively grant ownership of concepts, rather than tangible creations. This is damaging for innovation because companies like Apple and Google often file patents for ideas in which they made no investment and which they may never pursue. High margins would typically attract competitors—but the patent system makes any potential investor in genuine innovation very wary, for fear of litigation.

Before I sign on the dotted line . . .

☐ *Who owns the intellectual property created by this contract?*

☐ *Is intellectual property ownership a real issue in a specific requirement? Or is there a not wholly informed approach that the customer should own everything, simply because they're paying the supplier?*

☐ *Is a separate license agreement a better way to handle the intellectual property?*

☐ *What monetary value should be placed on the intellectual property?*

Termination

Termination provisions are included in contracts to specify when and why the contract can be ended early. These clauses are usually divided into **termination for cause** and **termination for convenience**.

Termination for convenience essentially allows a party to terminate a contract simply because it no longer suits their purposes. Generally, the buyer will not allow the seller to terminate for convenience. Buyers generally insist that only they are allowed to terminate for convenience. The key negotiating points in a termination for convenience clause are the amount of notice required, details of unwinding the contract, and, of course, compensation.

Termination for cause provisions include the specific reasons for which either party may end the contract. Sellers typically insist that the contract may be ended in the event of non-payment or bankruptcy. It is not uncommon to have a *force majeure* basis for termination, which is triggered when a major event outside the seller's control makes performance impossible.

Buyers often insist on the ability to terminate the contract for any significant breach by the seller. This would generally center on a failure of the seller to perform as contracted, but could also include a bankruptcy or change in ownership of the seller.

The compensation for a termination for cause generally specifies that the terminating party is entitled to specific types of damages. The amounts and types of damages are frequently negotiated and should be adequate and reasonable in relation to the nature of the contract.

Depending on the nature of the services being provided the customer should consider having a contractual provision enabling them to 'step in' and take over the service if the supplier is not performing. The customer should consider carefully the operational impact of a contract being terminated. Does the service need to continue, while not using the contracted supplier? If so, how can this be done practically as well as contractually?

Developing a Statement of Work

A Statement of Work (SOW) is a document describing the essential functional and technical requirements for services, including the standards that will be used to determine whether the requirements have been met. It should identify measurable or verifiable performance and acceptance criteria; such criteria minimize any uncertainty about whether work has been satisfactorily completed.

This document is generally an exhibit (appendix) to a service contract that specifies terms relating to the provision of services in general. If special terms and conditions were needed for particular work engagements that differed from the services contract they would be specified within the SOW.

A SOW may be simple or complex, flexible or definitive, depending on what it describes. It can be as simple as a 'remove lawn debris' description, or as complex as the specific requirements for a software development, an outsourced business process, or a new building. In many instances the complexity of the SOW may in fact have all of the elements of a services contract.

Like any piece of writing that conveys information and explains ideas, a good SOW must be well organized. It must educate those who read it by moving from things generally understood to the exceptional items, from the commonly known to the highly specialized.

It is as important to the supplier as it is to the customer that the agreement for work performed is formalized in a legally binding document. Within the document it is imperative that control mechanisms such as acceptance criteria or service levels are documented to ensure successful completion of the project.

The SOW generally represents a working document that will be used by many different parties to oversee and manage the transaction. Clarity, simplicity and thoroughness are key attributes to minimize confusion and dispute and to provide a good baseline for assessment of change.

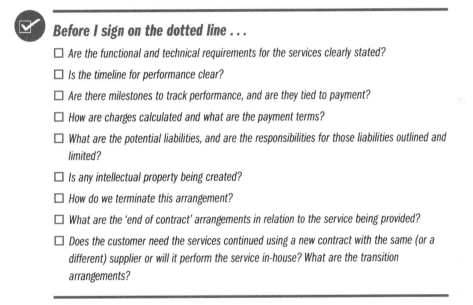

Before I sign on the dotted line . . .

☐ Are the functional and technical requirements for the services clearly stated?

☐ Is the timeline for performance clear?

☐ Are there milestones to track performance, and are they tied to payment?

☐ How are charges calculated and what are the payment terms?

☐ What are the potential liabilities, and are the responsibilities for those liabilities outlined and limited?

☐ Is any intellectual property being created?

☐ How do we terminate this arrangement?

☐ What are the 'end of contract' arrangements in relation to the service being provided?

☐ Does the customer need the services continued using a new contract with the same (or a different) supplier or will it perform the service in-house? What are the transition arrangements?

11.3 Contracts for the sale of both goods (products) and services

Logically and simply stated, a contract for the sale of both goods (products) and services should contain the essential elements of both contract types.

A good sales and service agreement will clearly define exactly what goods are being bought and sold as well as the specific services to be performed. The same standards for the detailed information to be included in this type of contract apply. Distinctions occur when terms must be different because of the inherent differences between products and services.

Price and payment terms

The combined contract must address the unique terms for both products and services. While a common payment term may be used that simply states that payments are to be made within 30 days of the date of invoice, that clause resolves none of the issues as to how the invoice is to be calculated, on what it may be based, or when it may be issued.

Many combined agreements will have attachments that reflect current pricing for products, including units of measure, taxes, duties and other costs for goods, and will have the specific service costs included in the statement of work. This separation is particularly important if acceptance criteria are required for either the goods or services or both.

Warranty and remedy

Warranties are the guarantees that whatever is purchased in the contract will be as it was described. Remedies are the options available to correct any deficiencies.

Warranties on goods are generally that the product will perform according to the product specifications published by the seller. These are sometimes reproduced within the contract itself, although more frequently they are simply referenced. Detailed product specifications can be very voluminous. Buyers typically want any specifications that were developed as part of the RFx process to be within the warranty, particularly if a standard product is modified for their purposes.

The most common warranty for services is that the work will be performed in a 'professional and workmanlike manner'. Courts generally interpret this to mean that the work should be of the same quality as that performed by another professional in the same specialty.

Combination contracts often go beyond products and services and into the gray area where services essentially become products. The end-product of a combination contract may well be a piece of custom developed software or a report for a regulatory agency. In this instance elements of a product warranty may be appropriate. Combination contracts must clearly state that a different warranty applies to a deliverable if that is negotiated.

Remedies for a breach of a product warranty are easily remembered as 'the three Rs' for Replace, Repair, or Refund. Contracts will specify which of these apply, the order in which they may be invoked, and which party chooses the remedy. Sellers will usually retain the right to determine how any warranty claim is resolved.

Remedies for a failure to perform services are slightly more limited. Either the services may be performed again, or a refund may be offered. Again the contract should specify which party chooses the remedy.

Liability

A liability is a legal responsibility or obligation to pay or do something. Combination contracts often address certain aspects of liability in a joint manner, but frequently have separate specific sections related to the individual products and services.

Common provisions include limitation of overall liability, whether the limit is 'per occurrence' or aggregate, and the type of damages that will be paid.

The first issue of liability most contracts address is the limitation of liability. This is a frequently negotiated clause. The purpose is to limit the total financial obligation (or risk exposure) of both parties. This is generally expressed as a figure that relates to the total value of the contract; this may or may not reflect the actual risk exposure, particularly if a low cost item is being purchased as a component of an expensive product to be resold. In these cases an amount unrelated to contract value might be more appropriate.

Buyers will frequently want any liability limits to be on a 'per incident' or 'per occurrence' basis. This means that each time there is a product failure the buyer can recover damages up to the limitation. Sellers obviously seek to limit total exposure. This will often lead to a contract with two limitations stated. One is a limit on the value of any single claim; the second is an aggregate or total limit for all claims under a contract.

Direct damages are the easiest to determine. This is a loss that occurs directly as a result of the contract. If a buyer purchases a box of 100 ink pens and finds that ten of them do not work, the direct damage would be the value of those ten pens.

Beyond direct damages, most buyers seek to recover some of the other costs that relate to a product or service failure. These are often referred to in the general category of 'indirect damages' and include consequential, incidental and special damages.

- **Consequential damages** are those that occur as a result of or as a consequence to the contract. These are often disputed and subject to differences of interpretation. They must 'flow from the contract breach' and must be able to have been foreseen by a reasonable person.
- **Incidental damages** refer to those losses that are related to caring for the goods after the contract has been breached by either the buyer or seller. The 'cost of cover' or the re-procurement of goods falls into this category and is often a costly item.
- **Special damages** compensate for extra costs incurred by the non-breaching party such as extra costs for repairs, loss of irreplaceable items, etc.

Contracts in many industries, particularly high-tech, often list different types of losses that may occur such as loss of data, breaches of privacy, or breach of regulatory guidelines, and then may specify whether or not damages will be paid.

Often it is not easy to specify exactly the value of a loss or contract breach. This is handled by specifying an amount that is called a liquidated damage which is payable instead of calculating the actual damage. The liquidated damage amount is negotiated by the parties and is identified separately in the contract. Legally liquidated damages are meant to be a genuine pre-estimate of likely loss and not a provision to penalize a supplier. In practice they are generally negotiated within standard company guidelines and considered as a penalty provision by the customer and a limitation of liability provision by the supplier.

It can be frightening to look at the different ways a supplier may encounter liability. There are physical third party liability risks where employees or products could cause physical damage to a buyer, their customers, or the general public, and so on. Failure of a product to perform may be the easiest liability to calculate.

It would not be possible to list a comprehensive set of liabilities that an organization could encounter. These vary significantly by industry as well as by the specific goods or services being covered by the contract.

Liabilities are an important part of managing business risk. Often, both parties will mutually exclude or limit certain liabilities to reduce unintended risk. Liability clauses in contracts can state the maximum damages either party is responsible for in breaches of the contract. It is important that the contract reflects the relative risk of damage for a breach.

The outcome of negotiations on limitation of liabilities may affect the purchase price of a product, the culture of the implementation (saving scores to be settled after contract signature) or even the willingness of either/both party to do business.

 ### Before I sign on the dotted line . . .

☐ Are the functional and technical requirements for both products and services clearly stated?

☐ Is the timeline for performance and/or delivery clear?

☐ How are charges calculated and what are the payment terms? Is there a distinction between products and services?

☐ Is liability clearly addressed and limited?

☐ Is any intellectual property being created?

☐ What is the warranty for the products and services?

☐ How do I walk away if I need to?

11.4 Summary

Contracts should never be developed in isolation or without direct reference to the specific transaction or relationship they are covering. Today's focus on compliance and control has resulted in a template-driven world where more than 90 percent of businesses operate with a portfolio of standard contract forms. While these can considerably reduce the time and risk associated with contracting, they do not remove the responsibility of those involved with the deal to apply their intelligence to underlying suitability. This may mean a specific transaction or relationship needs additional terms, amended terms or deleted terms.

Intellectual property issues are common in services agreements, and the parties need to be aware of the contract terms regarding the ownership of anything created under the contract. Most technology companies have standard policies governing this topic, and when situations demand a different approach the parties must handle the requirement as creatively as possible.

Simply understanding the terms written in the contract is not sufficient, as was discussed earlier in the book. Many terms are included in contracts by operation of law.

The growth of universal or consolidated standards continues, although slowly. There is growing consensus at both international and regional levels over standards for services, software, intellectual property rights, and in key areas like competition law, which can have a dramatic impact on the commercial process.

The concerns raised in this section are not unique to a single type of contract. Awareness of the issues helps to achieve clarity in the overall transaction.

CHAPTER 12

DEVELOP PHASE: LICENSES AND LEASES

All business success rests on something labeled a sale, which at least momentarily weds company and customer.

Tom Peters

Licenses and leases are similar to contracts for sale. Licenses differ in that the property is intangible, and there is no transfer of ownership. Leases also do not provide for a transfer of ownership, but they are distinguished from licenses by always having a specific end date or term.

Commercial contracts for licensing are most often related to software; leasing contracts are generally related to real property or financing for capital expenditures, and they will be the area of focus for this chapter.

It is worth noting that software once again offers a clear example of an area where the nature of the offering—and hence of the underlying contract—has evolved substantially in recent years. 'Click-wrap' agreements and software-as-a-service are the new models that have evolved from the early days of term and perpetual licenses. The rights and charging principles vary substantially, with software-as-a-service essentially making the software into a utility, often delivered through a third party 'cloud' provider. As contracts change to keep pace with technology and new business models we will continue to see licenses struggle to keep pace with the times.

12.1 *Licenses*

It is essential to understand the important concept of licensing, where a supplier retains ownership of the software code but allows its use under certain conditions described in the licensing terms. The licensing terms become paramount to describe how the software can be used and under what conditions.

Definitions

It is relatively standard practice for software licenses to begin with a series of definitions. Technology contracts in general are often subject to misinterpretation as the common use of specific terms changes over time. The list of definitions varies by license, but there are a few terms that are consistently important for users to understand.

The first term that must be understood is **Authorized User**. There should be a clear definition of who is considered a user of the software. The cost of the software may be based on the number of users, so from

that perspective this is a key term, but from a business use perspective any restrictions must be delineated. For example, must an individual be an employee to be authorized to use the software? Companies frequently use contractors and sometimes provide customer offerings where the end customer uses software. Restricting use to employees may, therefore, be problematic. A sufficiently broad definition of this term can generally be negotiated if the company assumes responsibility for the actions of the authorized users.

Hardware is usually a very straightforward definition. It is common for all types of equipment or hardware to be itemized by type and serial number. This identified hardware is where the software is installed.

The location where the software is physically located is usually defined as a **Site**. This is also where the users may access the software. *Site* is a significant term because as businesses change and expand there may be a need to have software located outside the country where it was originally licensed. Suppliers may often require additional payments for this flexibility, particularly if the new location poses additional intellectual property risks for the software. This dimension may become more complex with the need for customers to have disaster recovery facilities and also the use of cloud computing platforms to provide hardware and network capacity.

Software is continually being revised and improved, and there is a series of specialized terms related to these enhanced versions. These terms may vary by the software manufacturer, particularly with respect to what versions require the payment of additional license fees. In general, a **Major Release** is a version of the software that contains new functionality and usually combines any previous versions. A number to the left of a decimal point (i.e. 2.0 to 3.0) indicates a major release. A **Minor Release** is a version of the software that contains minor enhancements. A number to the right of a decimal point (i.e. 2.3 to 2.4) indicates a minor release.

There is also a distinction between an Update and Upgrade. An **Upgrade** is usually a new version of the software with new functionality. An **Update** is software generally provided to fix bugs and make small corrections, but does not usually contain material changes.

Individual updates are often issued by way of a **Patch**. Updates are generally provided at no charge, but there may be a fee for upgrades.

License types

There are many varieties of software licenses, but the two major distinctions are the permitted uses of the software and term of usage.

The most common types of licenses are:

- **Perpetual licenses**—the customer has the right to use the software in accordance with the license restrictions for an extended period of time. This can be interpreted in different ways, but generally means never ending.
- **Term licenses**—the customer has the right to use the software for the duration of the contract only
- **Shared licenses**—this may arise where there is joint ownership of the intellectual property rights in the commissioned or bespoke work. The parties may agree that one party owns the full rights in the commissioned work but the other party is granted an unlimited license to further develop and enhance the commissioned work without permission from the party that owned the original copy.
- **Third party license rights**—whereby the subcontractors or agents of the customer will have access to the software provided confidentiality agreements are put in place and the software is not licensed to competitors of the supplier.
- **Short evaluation licenses**—where software is evaluated for 30 to 90 days without the payment of a license fee.
- **Click-wrap or shrink-wrap licenses**—these are more common where off-the-shelf software is provided rather than bespoke or specially commissioned software.
- **Freeware or open source licenses**—this is an inexpensive way to obtain robust software but the supplier will need to ensure that the specific requirements of each software license has been fulfilled so that the supplier's proprietary software does not itself become 'open source'. In addition, the supplier must pass on to the customer the open source software or freeware terms and conditions in the contract.

To avoid major arguments during the relationship, it is important to define what is meant by 'perpetual' or 'term' license, to identify the

license restrictions and to ensure that contract terms and conditions specify the expectations of both customer and supplier.

Terms of use

The **term** or **scope of use** is at the core of software licensing terms and conditions. Software companies are reluctant to give the customer unlimited use of software without charging substantial licensing fees. Generally the fewer restrictions on use (unlimited hardware, unlimited sites, unlimited users) the higher the license fee. How use is granted is one key element that directly affects the price of the deal.

The Scope of Use or License Grant describes the ways in which customers can use the software. Software use is generally limited to internal business purposes. It does not typically allow the customer to use the software for the benefit of other companies. Some licenses offer the customer the ability to make changes, customizations, or modifications. There are typically restrictions on how this must be done, ownership of the intellectual property, and reductions in warranty or support. The license terms usually prohibit certain activities such as resale or redistribution, reverse engineering, decompiling, or publishing benchmark data.

Freeware or open source licenses may not cost money, but this does not mean they are free from restrictions. These licenses allow users to modify the products and redistribute the new products, but generally those new products must also be provided at no charge and must allow other users free access to the developed code. Incorporating software licensed under these terms into an otherwise proprietary product may void all commercial benefits in the software.

Assigning the right to use

Continuing with the theme of usage rights, the parties must address future uses and changing circumstances in the contract. Most companies change their structure over time. Between spin-offs, divestitures, and acquisitions, the corporate landscape can change dramatically. Terms and conditions must be included that address these situations; the supplier will need to anticipate the demands from the customer to continue use. The type of use that is permitted will depend upon the type of corporate change. Unlimited assignment of rights to use of the software is difficult for vendors when ownership changes or ceases to exist; such an assignment means that software or other valuable intellectual property is subject to use by future and unknown successors to the existing customer. The supplier may need to consider use of a restricting clause prohibiting assignment of such intellectual property to known competitors.

Customers may also become subject to two different license agreements when acquiring companies that use the same software. While smoothing other integration issues, combining the agreements and maintaining the value of each can be difficult.

Sometimes the customer may want to outsource the use of the software to a third-party service provider or allow contractors to use the software on their behalf by including rights to do this in the contract. The supplier will need to consider the position and rights that it wants to take in such a situation. Suppliers of software think very carefully before allowing access to key intellectual property, especially if access is provided to competitors and there is a risk of endangering the supplier's position in the marketplace by making the software available to third parties.

As with most terms in commercial contracts, a central issue is cost. Some vendors choose to charge for any privilege of assignment. Other vendors may view this as an opportunity to expand future business. Customers need assurances that they will be able to continue to use software, particularly mission-critical software, during corporate transitions. This requires a negotiated balancing act between flexibility and protection of intellectual property assets.

Maintenance

Software licenses are unique in that they frequently include the terms for 'maintenance'. Software maintenance services are usually considered to be a type of hybrid, combining both the provision of professional services and also future enhancements to the software.

Maintenance services can be delivered as part of the original contract and can also continue to be a delivery requirement after the rest of the contract is complete and has terminated. There is usually a section addressing ongoing software maintenance during the life of the contract and another section addressing any maintenance of software services

where the contract has terminated. The parties should also address the situation where the supplier becomes insolvent, in which software source code escrow arrangements will become important. With these arrangements, a trusted third party ensures access to the source code if the supplier becomes unable to support its software.

Maintenance pricing is a significant factor in the total cost of ownership for the customer as well as being a significant revenue source for the vendor. Maintenance pricing, terms and conditions will often be a separate section in a contract. Maintenance terms should include what kind of maintenance will be provided by the supplier and under what circumstances.

Maintenance costs can be calculated in many ways; frequently they are a percentage of the purchase price, and future licenses impact future maintenance. The customer should be aware of the potential for increases in these fees and may want to negotiate limits on increases beyond its control. The price of maintenance is increasingly negotiable. Major suppliers have traditionally resisted flexibility, but they are open to exploring alternatives that may vary the percentage charged.

Beyond the costs, there are several terms that should be clarified. First, there is the question of support and how it will be delivered. Software maintenance generally includes telephone support assistance by the supplier, electronic self-help (usually via a website), and perhaps even on-site visits for more serious issues. The terms should define service levels and set expectations for the maintenance program.

The start date for maintenance differs among vendors. Some suppliers begin maintenance when the warranty period ends (usually 30 to 90 days after delivery or acceptance). Others begin maintenance on the day the software is delivered. Increasingly, large customers may have a policy about when maintenance should start and end; they may demand the ability to 'synchronize' the maintenance term with their own internal calendar, or to be synchronized with other product schedules, especially if the software is part of an integrated solution.

The customer will also need to understand the differences in releases, updates, upgrades, and fixes to know which are included in maintenance and which are subject to additional charges. Policies on upgrades vary significantly among suppliers and have created customer concerns. The customer should also know about any requirements to install the current release or to be within a limited number of releases to continue receiving maintenance protection. The supplier may require this, to ensure the right level of resource is applied to provide maintenance and to ensure the software is stable, given the constant changes in technology. The cost impact should be explored as much as is possible to avoid costly release updates that have no clear economic value to the customer.

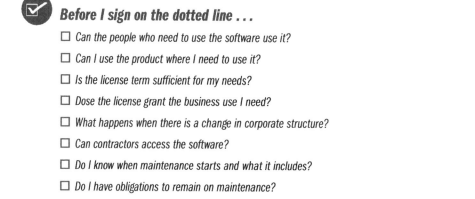

Before I sign on the dotted line . . .

☐ Can the people who need to use the software use it?

☐ Can I use the product where I need to use it?

☐ Is the license term sufficient for my needs?

☐ Dose the license grant the business use I need?

☐ What happens when there is a change in corporate structure?

☐ Can contractors access the software?

☐ Do I know when maintenance starts and what it includes?

☐ Do I have obligations to remain on maintenance?

☐ Are license fees and maintenance fees clearly listed so I know what the cost is today and in the future?

12.2 Leases

A lease is similar to a license in that there is no transfer of ownership, but it must be for a fixed term with a specific end-date, and payments are regularly made throughout its term. Leases are often used as a mechanism to finance purchases.

In addition to a fixed term, a lease will identify the property being leased, provide any conditions of renewal, specify the amount and frequency of the rental payments, list default conditions, and detail any

security deposits and conditions for the return of the property. The lease will also address any restrictions on the use of the property and specify insurance coverage and responsibility for required maintenance.

Leases for non-real property fall broadly into two different types: operating leases and finance leases. There are different financial terms to the leases, but they also receive different accounting treatment and serve different business purposes.

Finance lease

A finance lease is a commercial arrangement where a finance company purchases an asset but allows a lessee to have use of the asset during the term of the lease. The lessee pays rent during the term, which allows the finance company to recover the cost of the asset and earn interest. The term of the lease is normally the same as the useful life of the equipment. At the end of the lease the lessee usually has the option to acquire ownership by payment of a predetermined fee.

The finance company, or lessor, is the legal owner of the asset during the term of the lease, but the lessee has control of the asset. The way this is expressed for accounting purposes is that the lessee has 'substantially all of the risks and rewards' of ownership.

The accounting impact of this type of transaction varies internationally. While there is no universal standard, in general the following principles apply.

A finance lease is capitalized, so both assets and liabilities increase on the balance sheet.

Expenses for a finance lease are allocated between interest expense and principal value in the same way as a loan.

Operating lease obligations are not recognized on the balance sheet. They are operating expenses deducted from profits.

Rules classifying leases as financial leases or operating leases are more rigid in the US than in other regions.

Operating lease

The term of an operating lease is short compared to the useful life of the asset being leased. It is commonly used to acquire equipment on a relatively short-term basis. The monthly rental does not generally cover the cost of the asset.

Operating leases are used for expensive industrial equipment. This has become a cost-effective way for the outsourcing of industrial equipment. It allows the company to use its equity for its core business rather than tying it up in an equipment investment that produces no direct added value.

Ownership of the asset does not pass to the lessee at the end of an operating lease.

Accordingly, at the end of an operating lease, the lessee must determine what action it will take with respect to the equipment. Generally, one of the following will occur:

- Return of the equipment to the lessee
- Renewal of equipment lease
- Purchase of equipment at its market value.

The principal advantage to an operating lease is its lack of impact on the balance sheet. Rents are usually operating expenses that are deducted from profits, and cash flow may be improved. Tax treatment of operating leases may be favorable depending on the jurisdiction.

Real property

Leases of real property are often called 'tenancies' and are the subject of considerable differences in local and regional laws. Unlike other contracts where the applicable law may be chosen, the local law normally governs leases.

A lessee is obligated for the rental amount for the full term of the lease whether or not they use the property for the full term. At the conclusion of the initial term of the tenancy the property is usually vacated, but tenancy may continue on a basis considered to be 'at will' or month to month until notice is given by either party.

Before I sign on the dotted line ...

☐ Is the item being leased clearly identified?

☐ What is the term of the lease?

☐ How much is the rental?

☐ At the end of the lease what happens to the asset?

☐ Am I responsible for insurance and maintenance?

☐ How will this be shown in my financial statements?

12.3 **Summary**

Many of the terms in licenses and leases are similar to those found in contracts for the sale of goods and/or services. While this chapter focuses on the software aspect of licensing, that is not its only application. Common business practices such as franchises, publication, and character merchandising are all aspects of licensing. Licensing has become in many areas a legal sub-specialty that focuses on the need to match contract law with intellectual property law to facilitate business objectives.

Software licenses will always evolve, struggling to keep pace with ever changing technology and business models.

Leases are generally for real property. Their use has expanded into financial leases for capital expenditures and operating leases for equipment. Often the choice to lease instead of buy equipment is motivated by a desire to have the transaction reflected positively on financial reports.

CHAPTER 13

DEVELOP PHASE: OTHER BUSINESS RELATIONSHIPS

You can't stay in your corner of the Forest waiting for others to come to you. You have to go to them sometimes.

A. A. Milne

Previous chapters have focused on the sales process. In the commercial world business relationships do not always involve the provision of goods and services to each other. Contracts play a different role in these relationships as they define how the companies will work together to either 'sell through' one another or 'sell with' one another.

Because of this fundamental difference in purpose, the terms in these contracts are very different from sales contracts. The key elements for these agreements still rely on a clear description of exactly what each party will do under the agreement, the financial commitments of the parties, and how the success of the relationship will be evaluated.

Before appropriate terms can be established, it is critical to determine the type of relationship that will best fit the capabilities and goals of the parties. This chapter investigates partnerships, alliances and distribution, and the related competition rules and laws to be aware of when entering into a relationship.

In this chapter, we will examine the common contractual partnering and aligning relationships and laws controlling them. These are broadly classified into two categories. The first category is agreements where one company essentially sells 'through' another. The second category describes agreements where two or more companies agree to sell 'with' each other.

13.1 *Working with agents and distributors*

Many companies use agents, resellers, representatives and distributors to help in generating sales or performing services in international market segments or countries. Reasons for this vary from familiarity with local business practices to cost-effectiveness. These channels expand the market for goods and services through previously established relationships and by offering incremental value such as specialized services and localizations that benefit local consumers.

- A company may need a subsidiary, joint venture or other direct means of marketing and supplying products and services within a particular country or territory.

- There may be special relationships that are required or helpful to do business in a particular market, such as trading with some Middle Eastern countries that require business to be handled through a local agent or distributor.

Establishing third party channels of this type is not a straightforward decision and results in significant business consequences. Although at one level it may expand and complement marketing efforts, at another it places severe restraints on freedom of action in the market. For example, direct sales to customers may not be possible in specific territories; flexibility in negotiating prices is lost; obligations to use the channel may exist even when customers want a different approach. Understanding agency/distribution principles and laws is essential for good business decision-making.

The key distinction between an agent and a distributor is that an agent is a representative of the principal company while a distributor is an independent entity. In an agency relationship the customer may remain with the principal, but a distributor controls its own customers.

A distributor not only possesses the goods being sold, but also takes title to them. An agent holds the goods temporarily (or may take orders that are then fulfilled directly by the manufacturer), but does not own them. The distributor is acting on its own behalf, usually by purchasing the goods from the manufacturer, adding a profit margin and reselling the goods. *Any attempts to set or influence distributor sales prices are in most cases illegal and breach competition laws in most major jurisdictions.*

The legislative environment governing these relationships is complex and varied. It is also critical to understand whether there are potential issues under relevant bribery and corruption laws (e.g. the UN Convention against Corruption and the OECD Convention on Bribery of Foreign Public Officials in International Business Transactions, the US Foreign Corrupt Practices Act, Anti-Bribery Act etc.). Historically, local third party agreements were used to pay 'commissions' or 'facilitation payments' to key decision-makers, especially in government contracts. In some markets, pressure for such activity remains strong and must be avoided. To maintain corporate integrity, agents and distributors should be asked to provide references and financial information as well as certifications that they have read and agreed to relevant policies, laws, and export controls.

Decisions about agent/distributor agreements are always influenced by business objectives and market circumstances. The following list covers major concerns for most of these agreements:

- Consider the distributor's distribution channels and capabilities to move products.
- Authorized territory—this may be geographic or based on a market segment (e.g. the country of France, any company with less than 100 employees, pharmaceutical companies only). In many situations—especially within the European Union because of the single market principle—it may not be possible to impose restrictions.
- Minimum amounts of sales or purchases required from the agent/ distributor to have the agreement renewed. This is not acceptable in some regions.
- Performance terms, such as training personnel and marketing budgets. Non-performance by the agent/distributor should be linked to cause for termination.
- For distributors, price provisions—what they will pay for goods, or the discount(s) they receive from standard prices.
- For agents, the basis of their commission structure, and expenses limitations.
- For agents and distributors outside the country, currency fluctuation.
- Start and end dates.
- Stock holding / inventory obligations and handling of returns. What happens to 'old' product, for example when you discontinue or introduce a revised product line? What happens on termination?
- Obligations to provide services, such as customer support, warranty.
- Quality obligations—type of premises required, staff training etc.
- Confidentiality policies, handling of confidential information and trade secrets.

13.2 *Location really matters*

Global variations in laws about relationships with third parties

At least 32 countries worldwide and 14 states in the US have laws affecting relationships with agents, representatives and distributors. It is very important that these are analyzed before entering into a relationship with a third party because they impose very real limitations on the supplier's future freedom of action. The best time to think about the relationship is before it begins, because the objectives and circumstances of the parties usually change over time.

Competition law with third party agreements

Competition law has been mentioned briefly, and most countries regulate anti-competitive aspects of these arrangements. This is called vertical restraint in the EU. Price fixing agreements are almost universally prohibited. Depending upon the circumstances direct or indirect non-compete obligations are prohibited.

Law may also restrict territory establishment, essentially limiting the ability to grant distribution rights. For example, both Indonesia and Bahrain allow a foreign company to appoint only one agent to represent a particular type of business. In many of the Middle Eastern countries, the agent or representative must be a local citizen. Saudi Arabia prohibits direct sales and requires that a local representative is used to make all sales. Exclusive territories within the EU are often problematic as a distributor granted rights to sell in one country couldn't generally be excluded from another without violating anti-trust laws.

Competition law is a sub-specialty, and generalizations and simplification can prove costly. It is always prudent to have a specialist in this area to review business agreements for compliance with local laws.

Terminating an agreement with agents or distributors

No discussion of local laws would be complete without reviewing termination. Almost all countries and many states have laws governing the ability to terminate a contract with an agent or distributor, even if the contract is for a specified term. Countries and states enacted these laws to protect citizens from exploitation. Historically a company would hire an agent to get a 'foot in the door' in a new market and then terminate the agreement when the business became established. The agent had generally incurred expenses to establish the business, generate goodwill, or given up other profitable ventures.

These laws prevent a company from terminating an agreement without proof that the agent was in breach of its obligations. If this is not proven, there is liability for significant damages. Examples of this include:

- In Belgium, a distributor agreement cannot be terminated without paying a significant amount for the 'goodwill' the distributor has established. The termination payment may amount to two or three years of the distributor's income.
- In Belgium, two renewals of a distributorship contract constitute a contract for an indefinite duration.
- In Ecuador, only the representative has the right to terminate.
- In Thailand, companies are obliged to continue commission payments to local representatives for several years after termination.
- Honduras provides for five years of gross profit or five times average gross profit if the distribution contract is less than five years.

13.3 Selling with business consortia, joint ventures and alliances

The size and complexity of certain projects has led to the development of the sales consortium as an alternative to bidding on a project individually. This is often seen in construction and development. In this model the suppliers and the construction contractor assume joint responsibility to the customer and share responsibility with one another. This is a method of bidding that has become increasing popular for turnkey or other large contracts or where the project risk is too great to be reasonably assumed by a single entity.

A **consortium** is defined as: *An alliance between companies by which, in tendering for a project, they make clear to the customer that it is their desire to work together, and that their tenders have been coordinated on that basis.* The companies usually exercise a great deal of care to make

sure that their individual offers are such that they dovetail together and collectively comprise a complete scheme. In the US a consortium is seen almost exclusively in alliances between not-for-profit research entities and for-profit companies. The for-profit company contributes money in exchange for rights in the intellectual property that is developed.

A **joint venture** is closely related to a consortium. Joint ventures are more commonly found in the US than elsewhere because business laws defining them are more formalized than in other regions. Having said that, there are many joint ventures formed internationally because of the great benefits received by companies located in developing economies. These governments offer substantial incentives to global companies to create local joint ventures.

Many people use the terms *consortium*, *alliance*, and *joint venture* interchangeably to describe the relationship whereby two or more companies pursue work together. There are significant legal differences among these terms, and some companies choose one term as a corporate convenience to refer to any similar endeavor. It is important to note that a true joint venture is implemented through a new entity in which a company and other parties make an equity (ownership right) investment.

Customers will generally require that the companies involved in any of these relationships give a joint warranty that the project will be complete and will operate satisfactorily. In most cases there is a statement that the members of the consortium/alliance /joint venture are jointly and severally liable to the customer. This means that each member of the team is legally responsible to the customer for its scope and the scope of each of the other members. The customer may choose to legally pursue one, some, or all of the consortium members regardless of who may be allegedly at fault. The consortium agreement is entered into to apportion this responsibility and set out the other rules that will govern the members of the consortium.

Because of the risks assumed in this business model, these contracts devote extensive attention to the management and allocation of risk. These contracts will have extremely detailed provisions including:

- Scope of work
- Responsibility for claims
- Proportionate value
- Limitation of liability
- Nature of the relationship
- Managing the consortium
- Resolution of disputes
- Engineering services
- Bid preparation

Case study: Moving from conflict to collaborative sharing of risk and reward

The UK's offshore wind farms represent an area of high opportunity but substantial risk. They demand initial high levels of investment and will require continued technological advance. At present, development is delayed because suppliers are reluctant to build capacity and no one is willing to take on the risks of technological uncertainty (for example, dealing with the limited warranties or performance undertakings that manufacturers offer in such untested conditions).

The industry has a history of adversarial relationships, which is reflected in contracts and contracting processes that seek to allocate risk to the weakest parties and lead to a blame-based culture.

A UK government working group has tried to find ways of breaking this pattern. It concluded that progress depends on realizing a need for a fairer balance of risk, moving away from traditional turnkey projects and towards innovative forms of collaborative multi-partner' contracts. New approaches to bid and negotiation procedures would help by allocating the share of risk or gain on a formula related to the extent of influence and control, and the ability to bear the risk.

The question now facing the industry is whether it can develop a shared perspective on risk and reward, rather than the traditional allocation of risk to the weakest party.

With this type of arrangement, and especially in joint development agreements, protection of each company's proprietary and intellectual

property is a significant concern. The contract should specify the type of technology, training and other information to be received from each party and how confidential information will be handled. Often it may be necessary to specify that information will not be deemed confidential because you may wish to avoid the potential for subsequent lawsuits. Ownership for any intellectual property developed must be specified.

Business strategies frequently change, especially over time, and it is critical that any partnership such as these has a termination strategy defined in advance. In particular, it is critical that the partners agree how dissolution will occur, including disposition of assets/liabilities at that time.

A consortium has many issues that must be considered from a business perspective and then adequately addressed within the contract. There are often tax implications that influence the structure of the consortium/alliance/joint venture. Other financial incentives may come into play where certain subsidies are available for local companies.

Before I sign on the dotted line ...

☐ Is this an agreement of equals in terms of risks and responsibilities?

☐ Do I understand the significance of joint and several liability?

☐ Do I understand the financial strength of each prospective member?

☐ Can alliance members subcontract or otherwise assign responsibilities?

☐ Will the consortium arrangement be exclusive or are the parties free to bid on the project with other companies?

☐ Who is preparing the final bid and who is paying the expenses to prepare it?

☐ How will this partnership be dissolved?

☐ How will proprietary information be handled and who owns developed intellectual property?

☐ How does program management relate to consortium management?

☐ Does this arrangement violate any regulatory issues such as export control or anti-trust?

☐ Are the companies compatible in terms of business practices and ethical standards?

13.4 *Prime/subcontractor agreements*

Prime/subcontractor agreements are another vehicle to assemble a complete solution to bid on a substantial and diverse project. The prime contractor has the direct relationship with the customer. The subcontractor has a contractual relationship only with the prime contractor. This approach is preferred over the previous arrangements when one company is performing a significant portion of the contract. Prime/subcontractor relationships are generally developed only for a single project.

A prime contractor is responsible to the customer for the entire scope of the project. It stands behind not only its own work but also that of its subcontractors. The project risk is managed differently from the consortium mode.

This contract arrangement uses what are often referred to as back-to-back agreements. These agreements should ideally be in place before submitting a bid to a customer; entering into obligations without 'back-to-back' commitments from subcontractors is a common source of contract failure. Appropriate non-disclosure agreements should be in place before sharing any information with a prospective teaming partner.

Because only the prime contractor is directly responsible to the customer, the subcontract must pass through or 'flow down' the appropriate requirements. In areas where the subcontractor is responsible for performance it must be aware of the contractual specifications.

 Case study: A poor subcontractor can cost you much more than money

Profits from Apple's iPhones and iPads have been achieved at too high a price for many consumers. The Californian company's reputation has been damaged by its Taiwanese manufacturer Foxconn, which is at the heart of a global scandal about dangerous factory conditions and long working hours.

Independent audits requested by Apple followed up on reports of suicides and abusive conditions at several of the Foxconn factories in China. The auditors found at least 50 violations of local regulations at Foxconn plants.

Apple has announced that it will pay Foxconn half the cost of improving its labor conditions, recognising that its customers will expect the company to make amends as a corporate social responsibility.

This is a change of mindset for Apple. Until recently the company had paid little attention to complaints from civil rights advocates and environmentalists about Foxconn's excessive overtime regime and unsafe working conditions. But now both Apple and its manufacturing partner realize that the resulting negative publicity and damaging impact on corporate reputation could have a huge impact on profitability.

The prime contractor usually leads on proposals prepared under this arrangement, with contributions from the subcontractor. Each company generally bears its own proposal costs.

It is important to note that prime/subcontractor arrangements are unique in that there are *two* contracts involved. There is the contract between the prime contractor and the customer and the contract between the prime contractor and subcontractor. The contracts must be carefully coordinated.

Before I sign on the dotted line . . .

☐ Is my company the only company that has a direct relationship with the customer?

☐ Is my company performing the majority of the work on this project?

☐ Does the contract with the subcontractor reflect all of the requirements of the prime contract?

☐ If I have a responsibility to the customer does the subcontractor have a similar obligation to me?

☐ Does the subcontractor have liability to me for its performance?

13.5 *Implementing alliances through teaming agreements*

Typically, a teaming agreement is a simple contract under which a company prepares a bid with one or more companies in order to respond to a Request for Proposal. A company and its team members have complementary capabilities (each adds something the other lacks), and by working together, seek to increase their chances of winning the bid.

Teaming may also take the form of joint advertising or promotion when a specific RFP has not been identified. Customers may sometimes request a teaming agreement to respond to a complex technical proposal.

A significant element of teaming agreements is the non-compete provision. Companies usually agree not to bid against each other during the teaming agreement; this provision is tailored in scope and duration for each agreement. Teaming agreements for a specific RFP generally limit competition for that opportunity only, while other arrangements may reflect more general marketing endeavors. Any non-compete provision generally lapses if the team has been eliminated from bidding.

If the team is successful in winning the bid, the teaming agreement is replaced by a prime contractor/subcontractor relationship.

Before I sign on the dotted line . . .

☐ *Are the responsibilities of each party detailed?*

☐ *Do I understand the restrictions on competition?*

☐ *When does the teaming agreement end?*

☐ *Are any follow-on contractual arrangements clearly understood?*

13.6 *A second relationship continuum*

Looking beyond the particular structure of a contractual relationship is often helpful from a business perspective. This can lead to better decision-making regarding the formalization of that relationship. In this view there are three basic levels of business relationships (Figure 13.1).

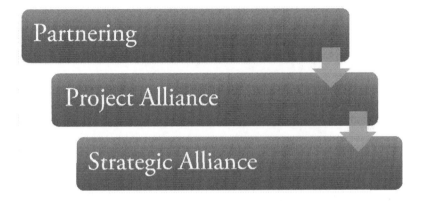

Figure 13.1   Three levels of business alliances

Partnering—sharing the project management responsibilities through open communication and shared objectives. This only works effectively when both parties have the same level of commitment. Having to define the commitment level in more detail can reduce this to a more traditional contract.

Project alliances—a time-based approach for a particular project and ends after the project is completed. The alliance is based on a mutually shared risk-and-reward scenario for both parties. This requires open-book accounting from both parties, with an agreement to put profit at risk and (usually) overheads too.

Strategic alliances—similar to project alliances but for a much longer commitment, usually a number of years. A typical example would be a long-term outsourcing relationship that provides goods or services in exchange for a guaranteed cash flow. The inherent benefit of a strategic alliance is that both parties will begin to understand each other's requirements and can institute continuous improvements to increase profitable returns in the future.

Relationship-based contracts between companies can ultimately strengthen the customer relationship. Effective agreements to sell through and with other entities, particularly local entities, provide better service and more complete solutions to end users.

13.7 Summary

Relationships are significant to the strategy of selling 'with' and 'through' others. These business relationships take on added importance in the international area. As with any contractual agreement, understanding the objectives for the relationship is key to success.

The terms in these contracts are different from sales contracts. The key elements for these agreements still rely on a clear description of the duties of each party, the financial commitments, and how the relationship will be evaluated.

CHAPTER 14

DEVELOP PHASE: COMPLEX AND SPECIALIZED AGREEMENTS

Life is really simple, but we insist on making it complicated.

Confucius

Global business has become increasingly complex, and customers are often seeking solutions that are too large for even giant companies to undertake on their own. This has led to highly specialized 'mega-deals' that incorporate all of the contracting elements contained within this Develop phase. Large teams of professionals from every business discipline usually structure these transactions.

The expertise required in these deals is beyond the scope of this book, but an awareness of the broad categories covered by these agreements is helpful as general business knowledge.

Agreements of this scale are generally found in one of three areas. Information Technology (IT) is the most familiar source of a 'mega-deal'. These transactions integrate hardware, software and services to provide a bundled solution to business problems. Large infrastructure projects combining architectural, engineering, and construction services is another area that produces very complex agreements. The most recent use of the mega deal is business outsourcing. ,

We are seeing an increased interest in contracting for situations where the desired outcome is known, but the means of getting there remain highly uncertain. Interestingly, as was recently observed by the CEO of Shell, this is creating growing interdependency between companies that have not previously worked especially closely. For example, no major building project today relies solely on the traditional construction companies; they have so much embedded technology that partnerships with the technology sector are fundamental to success.

14.1 *IT solutions*

IT solutions contracts differ from other types of arrangements because the buyer is relying on the supplier's expertise to design and integrate a full package of products, services, engineering, design, and consulting necessary to solve a business issue or problem. This may often include not just new products and systems but the integration with and/or transition from a customer's legacy systems.

IT solutions arrangements may include:

- Systems or network integration and management
- Managing and optimizing customer resources, facilities or networks
- Implementation and operations—for example, marketing, billing, distribution or inventory management systems

A key distinction in this type of contract is that the buyer gives up substantial control in specifying individual components of the solution. In many other types of arrangements, the buyer specifies what types of products and services are needed. In IT solutions contracts the buyer may only specify the problem needing resolution and relies totally on the supplier for its resolution. The supplier must provide the complete specifications for the work to be done.

As with any contract, the buyer must be certain exactly what it is buying. IT vendors have tended to use the term 'solution' to mean that the supplier provides the customer with a technical solution using the supplier's technology, which it will then integrate, deliver and install. Historically, the resulting contracts made little or no commitment to the interoperability of the component parts (e.g. hardware or software) and prices were based on the individual unit price lists—sometimes not even consolidated under a single invoice. The companies sold solutions, but delivered piece parts.

For a buyer, it is essential to understand what commitments are being made in terms of performance and interoperability. A true 'solutions' contract will establish clear liability on the supplier to ensure an effective solution; against this, the supplier must be able to rely on accurate and timely information from the buyer about the business environment and conditions within which the solution will operate.

14.2 *Major infrastructure*

Major infrastructure contracts have historically been complex because they incorporate many interdependent disciplines. Anyone who has done a home construction project has encountered on a small scale the difficulties confronted in large projects with complex schedules and large budgets. The size of these projects almost inevitably means that there will be problem areas identified in the contracts where abuse of the commercial process has occurred.

Public and private entities have frequently combined forces for infrastructure projects. This adds further complexity to an already cumbersome process.

 Case study: The Big Dig

Downtown Boston was the site of the most expensive highway project in the US. The official name was the Central Artery/Tunnel Project, but it was more widely known as the Big Dig. This megaproject in Boston rerouted the chief highway through the heart of the city, into a 3.5-mile tunnel. The project included the construction of a tunnel to improve access to the airport; it also included a bridge over the Charles River and a 1.5-mile series of public parks. Initially, the plan was also to include a rail connection between Boston's two major train terminals.

Planning for the project began in the 1970s but did not officially start until 1982. The project combined public and private interests by combining a highway improvement project with broad public support to a project to improve access to the airport that had strong business support.

Its complex beginnings did not bode well for the project, which faced ever increasing obstacles. Political and financial issues continued. Environmental and engineering problems followed closely. The construction itself encountered many problems from geological changes to archaeological findings.

Project management and oversight became muddled. The project was far too large for a single contractor, so the project was broken down into dozens of smaller contracts, which were still massive. The public transportation authority eventually combined some of its employees with the private joint venture employees in an integrated project organization. While this was intended to make management more efficient, it hindered the transportation authority's ability to independently oversee project activities. The public and private entities had effectively become partners in the project

Escalating costs, schedule overruns, leaks, design flaws, charges of poor execution, and the use of substandard materials plagued the Big Dig. There were even criminal charges and one fatality. The project was scheduled to be completed in 1998 at an estimated cost of $2.8 billion. The project was not completed until December 2007, at a cost of over $14.6 billion.

As a result of the fatality, leaks, and other design flaws, the consortium that oversaw the project agreed to pay $407 million in restitution, and several smaller companies agreed to pay a combined sum of approximately $51 million.

14.3 *Outsourcing*

The practice of outsourcing many functions or activities that had previously been performed internally by a company became widespread in the 1990s, especially in the US and parts of Western Europe.

Unlike procuring a supplier or subcontractor for a specific project, outsourcing gives the day-to-day operational control of a function or service to a specialist service provider who will be responsible for the provision of that service for a number of years.

It is common for the staff of the customer who previously provided the service in-house to be transferred to become permanent employees of the outsourcing organization. In such circumstances the existing employment rights and benefits of each member of staff would also transfer across to the outsourcer.

Outsourcing really began with IT and data processing services, but the significant growth in recent years has been in other areas such as logistics, human resources, and facilities management. Business process outsourcing (BPO) as this is known, could mean that functions or departments such as Training, Help Desk and Accounts and Finance move to an external service provider. In the technology sector areas such as application development, operation and maintenance of systems and networks and help desks may be outsourced.

The concepts of outsourcing have been tested and proven in the IT arena and now are being widely adopted in non-IT areas—often by the same companies that have proven them in the IT arena. New suppliers have stepped into the business process outsourcing arena and relatively low cost countries such as India and the Philippines are developing businesses that sell directly into the global marketplace.

This expansion has led to a significant amount of standardization in specific service segments, such as data-centers, desktop, telecommunications and server management as these sectors become mature. It also means many buyers have started to treat outsourcing as a commodity.

There are obvious areas such as security, disaster recovery and business continuity management which customers cannot afford to ignore in this transition to 'commodity purchasing'.

Standardization helps drive strong price competition and higher quality service levels. This makes outsourcing a more affordable approach even for small and medium size companies. Major suppliers such as IBM, HP and CSC remain essential for the 'mega-deal', especially in government and in industries that are restructuring, such as telecommunications, utilities and banking. In such deals, only those with significant funds and a wide risk portfolio can absorb the costs of bidding and the risks associated with performance.

Before I sign on the dotted line . . .

☐ *I will call the experts and take advantage of their knowledge and experience.*

14.4 Summary

Complex agreements are becoming increasingly common. We are seeing companies whose business model is entirely about creating and managing these large projects. As customers continue to look to share

their business risks there will be more companies who seek to profit from effectively managing that risk.

These agreements are individualized and very complex. They require incredible expertise to structure and manage. The risks are significant, but so is the potential for profit.

CHAPTER 15

NEGOTIATION PHASE: UNPLANNED NEGOTIATION

Be Prepared . . . the meaning of the motto is that a scout must prepare himself by previous thinking out and practicing how to act on any accident or emergency so that he is never taken by surprise.

Robert Baden-Powell

We have briefly reviewed the negotiation process earlier in the book and some ways to navigate it effectively. That may be somewhat remote from the real world that people face every day. Here, where the 'rubber meets the road' challenges are faced and often must be resolved on the spot. This frequently means little or no preparation time or consideration given to a negotiation style or framing approach. Often there are no goals, objectives, or guidance beyond an instruction to 'close the deal'.

The simple directive to close a deal might be sufficient. If the negotiator understands the transaction and is empowered with the necessary authority to modify a contract and ensure compliance with its terms, then this could be the fastest route to an agreement. However, too often the real world scenario is somewhat less than this ideal. Negotiators are more likely to be uncomfortable with some aspect of a transaction or to be unsure of approval authority or responsibility for compliance.

Journalists often refer to the '5 Ws and H' (Why, When, What, Who, Where, and How) to make certain that a newspaper article contains the essential factual elements. Clarity on the '5 Ws and H' can enable anyone to move closer to the fully empowered and confident negotiator.

Exactly Why, When, What, Who, Where, and How to negotiate varies among companies, individuals, and situations. This chapter explains how asking and answering these question prepares readers for the real world, on-the-spot negotiation. Thinking through the questions and answers is the best preparation for the unplanned negotiation.

15.1 Why negotiate?

Before stepping into any negotiation pause to ask *why* you are negotiating. There are many common reasons below, but understanding why you are being involved helps gauge the scope of action to pursue. Are you discussing money, providing clarity, or resolving a conflict? That answer helps you to respond appropriately, even 'on the fly'.

Money
The simple, and perhaps cynical, answer to "why negotiate?" is *money*. Companies and individuals negotiate because additional value is wanted

from a commercial transaction. Buyers may approach this from a perspective of wanting a lower price while sellers may approach it wanting to sell more units or obtain more favorable terms. Both parties see that there is some additional value to be gained, or there would be no negotiation. But money is not the only reason that people negotiate.

Clarity

The need for clarity can drive negotiation. One or both parties may pursue a negotiation to clarify an obligation or an intention, or to establish alignment between needs and capabilities. This may be prompted when one party feels that a contract clause is ambiguous or does not reflect the stated goals of the parties. Removing ambiguity from a document generally makes it better and more usable for the individuals who must actually perform the contract. This can be taken to an extreme position where one party seeks to document every possible contingency, making the document unduly long or obscuring the original intent. An overly prescriptive approach may also eliminate creativity and innovation, leading to poor performance and value over time.

 Case study: Buying a result or number of people?

A large hotel and casino complex outsourced its cleaning and maintenance services. The contract specified a minimum number of staff that must be deployed each day on cleaning duties. Over time, new technology and cleaning materials enabled the supplier to perform these duties with 25 percent fewer staff.

One day, the head of procurement received a call from the hotel's operations manager, demanding that payment should be withheld from the supplier, on the basis that the supplier was failing to send the specified number of staff and was therefore not in compliance with the contract. On questioning, the operations manager acknowledged that the quality of cleaning was entirely satisfactory and in accordance with service level standards.

As negotiated, the contract had offered no incentive for open discussion and sharing benefits from innovation.

Helpful contract language can alleviate the issue when the parties have an agreement on a particular term but one party feels the contract does not adequately reflect the intent. It can be useful to add clarifying language to the agreement and preface it with phrases such as "For the avoidance of doubt," or "By way of example only".

Where the ambiguity is found in a statement of work to be performed or a product description it must be resolved before the contract moves forward. This type of ambiguity goes to the heart of the deal itself. One party does not understand its obligations, which means the consideration the other party is anticipating is in jeopardy.

In the theoretical world a transaction does not get to the negotiation stage with any ambiguities at this level. In the real world it can and does happen. Indeed, IACCM research has indicated that the most frequent source of claims and disputes is disagreement over scope and goals. There is a real danger that, in their haste to close the deal and claim savings or commissions, negotiators may cut corners or avoid difficult conversations. This is why successful business and sustainable relationships depend on a willingness by both parties to ensure clarity of the requirements and obligations.

It may be necessary to expand the contract to detail the roles and responsibilities of each party. Again, this is a straightforward task if the parties have an agreement, but if there is no agreement then this could be contentious. At times the failure to understand responsibilities may be genuine, but at other times it may be used as a ploy to attempt to influence the price of the agreement. Questions such as, "You are providing the materials, right?" or "The price includes delivery, doesn't it?" that are raised after these points have been discussed and documented are generally attempts to gain a last-minute price adjustment. The best approach to this is often to point to the section of the contract or proposal where the issue is addressed.

Compliance

Compliance with internal policies, procedures, standards and systems can often compel negotiations. This happens increasingly when one or both parties have implemented enterprise resource planning (ERP) systems that may impose seemingly arbitrary standards on the business process. This additional complexity can seem insurmountable when there are competing ERP mandates on the part of both buyer and seller.

These issues arise even when there is fundamental agreement on the transaction itself.

 Case study: Do the requirements make sense?

The Chief Procurement Officer of an international mining company was visiting the company's facilities in a remote and undeveloped location. As part of the agreement with the national government, the company had invested micro-finance in local suppliers, most of whom had no business experience and could not read or speak English.

Before leaving, the CPO was reminded by his staff that local suppliers should sign the company's short-form agreement and that they must register onto the enterprise resource planning (ERP) system in order to be paid. These reminders were ringing in his ears as he drove to his first meeting, which was with the director of a start-up manufacturer of protective clothing. Through their interpreter, he soon gathered that the 50-page 'short agreement' was meaningless to the lady across the table; and as he glanced at the workers and realized there was no electric supply, he quickly concluded that the conversation about connecting to the ERP system might have little purpose.

While the mining company case study is an extreme example, our increasingly global dealings make the potential for fundamental mismatches more likely. In addition, the fact that so much negotiation today is virtual means that often we may lack the insights we need to understand fundamental issues or barriers to our assumed terms and conditions.

Resolving conflict

Most companies have internal standards and policies that have been adopted because they reflect an advantageous business model. These are often codified into a set of standard terms and conditions. In a negotiation the party that has the benefit of starting with its own standard terms is at an advantage when it comes to internal compliance. The buyer or seller who is working from the other's terms must evaluate the differences between two standards. The differences may be minimal or could reflect substantial issues; determining the extent of the differences is key to defining the scope of the negotiation and understanding the risks of non-compliance. Simply arguing which document will form the basis of the contract does not produce results.

Deviations from a corporate standard are not necessarily uncommon, particularly in rapidly changing industries where contract forms may not be regularly updated. Companies generally have provisions for common deviations, and have specifically designated approval authorities. As a negotiator it is important to understand exactly what terms may be changed and what approvals are required. Understanding the latitude to change terms empowers the negotiator.

Reviewing common goals, fallbacks, and walk away positions as discussed earlier gives a healthy foundation to enable individuals to step into negotiations without preparation.

Figure 15.1   Negotiation plan revisited

Opportunity

Perhaps the most exciting reason to negotiate is opportunity; realizing the potential growth in any transaction is an excellent motivator in negotiation. A common example is a volume pricing arrangement. A buyer wants to negotiate a better unit price while a seller wants to incentivize greater sales volume. A volume purchase agreement increases the amount of discount based upon sales volume. Both parties have increased opportunity.

Greater opportunity is also seen as buyers and sellers move along the relationship continuum discussed earlier. Moving from a transaction buyer to a relationship buyer is a process in which both buyer and seller must invest. It generally requires trust and confidence built upon a history of successful performance through which both parties have benefited.

 Case study: Obstacle or opportunity?

Company A provided complex seismic services to the oil and gas industry. This included the need to move high-value computers and software to the exploration and development location. Company A had developed an integration center in Texas to assemble the various elements of the eventual solution before shipping to the end-user location.

Company B was competing for the mainframe computer sales. Under its standard rules, equipment purchased in the US could not be shipped overseas. If they crossed US national borders, they lost all rights to warranty and support. It appeared that the customer need for central integration represented an impossible barrier until one of the negotiators suggested they should explore a consignment stock model, whereby the computer would be temporarily supplied to the Company A integration center, but Company B would retain title and then be responsible for the collection and shipment of the consolidated product to end user locations.

This solution added value for both sides because it meant that goods were shipped at transfer prices, saving almost 30 percent in import/export fees and taxes. In addition, Company B gained incremental revenue from the shipping services it provided. Overall, the parties were able to split the savings and each finished up about 15 percent better off.

15.2 *When to negotiate*

It may seem obvious, but if there is a reason to negotiate, it is an indicator that it might be an appropriate time to negotiate. If there is a deadline approaching such as the end of a fiscal year, budget period, or a project dependency there may be an urgency that spurs the negotiation. Both parties should be aware of time schedules that might provide an advantage. This is commonly seen when individuals wait until the end of a month or year to make a purchasing decision, and they are frequently rewarded with sales incentives.

Delays do not always result in price concessions; they can also mean that vendors may have price increases, or there may be cycles to the business that work against the buyer. For example, construction prices for labor are frequently lower in the winter when the supply of jobs is less, but they increase as the warm weather increases the seasonal demand.

Avoiding negotiation

It is as important to know when to avoid negotiation. Virtually everyone is familiar with the parent pushed to the edge of frustration by a child negotiating for something. At some point the parent explodes with one of two answers. The first is the predictable, "No because I am the parent and said so!" The second is the resigned, "Just go ahead and do what you want because I am tired of discussing it." While these two extremes are easily identifiable in this scenario, neither is really a desirable business outcome. Pushing beyond the common business boundaries to wear down the other party can result in the same outbursts from negotiating parties and damage longstanding relationships.

Avoid negotiating when tempers are high on either side. It is during these times that extreme positions are taken and parties may 'dig in' on an issue and refuse even reasonable or beneficial compromise. This sort of intractability is often best handled by taking a break and understanding that this is not the time to negotiate, despite other pressures.

Sensitivity to external factors is important in negotiation. Negotiators are people who confront personal crises while dealing with professional obligations. Personal issues such as illness, death and divorce will always affect a negotiation; business crises will also have an effect. It is not the time to negotiate when a partner has experienced a change in senior management, has announced significant reductions in force, or been the subject of adverse media attention. Negotiating a contract clause on data protection is never harder than immediately after a company has been in the press for security breaches.

Stepping back is sometimes necessary before stepping forward. Negotiation in the real world illustrates this dynamic. Finally, do not become ensnared by the belief that negotiation is somehow 'good'. In a perfect world, where there was complete alignment between a buyer's need and a seller's offer, there would be no need to negotiate. To that extent, negotiation actually represents a quality defect and efforts should be directed towards minimizing its need, not maximizing it.

Using power

Power is inherent in almost every interaction or negotiation, both internal (between stakeholders) and external. On a large scale this can be seen in the way that economically powerful areas such as the EU and North America wield power in treaties with less developed areas, or seek to impose regulatory authority on an international basis. But a negotiation occurs only when both parties see a reason or benefit to negotiation. Each has something the other wants—money, skills, knowledge, location, reputation, people, or products. This means that while there may be a disparity in power, both sides have power to some extent.

Power may be ***constructive***, meaning that it is the power to achieve a goal or need. It can also be ***obstructive***, preventing a goal from being realized. Urban renewal projects demonstrate this phenomenon. Developers buy distressed properties to begin renewal projects, and frequently pay much greater prices for the final parcels of land acquired. The owners of these parcels have obstructive power to prevent completion of the project. Property owners who are too resistant may lose that advantage if the developer exercises its power to walk away from the renewal project.

Both sides have power in a negotiation, and that power may shift during the course of the negotiation. A simple example of this can be seen in the procurement of accounting services. A company looks to change its accounting partner and may consider discussions with a large number of eager providers. It has flexibility, options, and power. Providers are vying for the opportunity. As time moves on, this power can erode. As the deadline looms for the transition, pressure increases to have a new provider under contract so there is continuity of service. The vulnerability of the procuring company increases each day, transferring the power in the negotiation to the provider.

It may seem obvious, but pressing any advantage in power makes it a better time to negotiate.

Renegotiation

Contracts generally have a term (a defined time period), and renegotiation is appropriate before any renewal or extension. This should not necessarily be viewed as the only time to negotiate. Ignoring business relationships except at contract renewal does not take advantage of changing market conditions or exceptional performance, both of which could trigger further negotiation. Significant changes to a scope of work should be a signal that discussions should be re-opened, if for no other purpose than assuring that clarity exists.

 Case study: Poor contracting carries a human cost

An Indian hospital had outsourced the supply and maintenance contracts for its gas pipeline system. A failure in oxygen supply resulted in the death of four patients.

The supply and maintenance of the hospital's gas pipeline had been contracted to an outside supplier since 1998. According to the supplier their operational contract expired in October 2011, but their maintenance contract continued until October 2012. The supplier had already started to reduce the number of staff deployed at the hospital and was threatening to withdraw all personnel. When the system started to malfunction, neither party took corrective action and one night a low-level technician found himself alone when oxygen supplies failed. Four patients were dead by the time normal supplies were restored.

The contract specified that an expert and a technician should be on site at all times. The hospital claimed that it had given verbal assurances of contract extension and that necessary funding had been sanctioned three weeks earlier.

The resulting dispute and 'blame game' demonstrated a fundamental lack of communication and contract management discipline. The consequences for both parties are severe: reputational damage and incremental costs, plus the likelihood that the relationship cannot be recovered. The result for the patients is, of course, even more severe.

15.3 *What to negotiate*

Price
Most negotiators focus first and foremost on price. The goal of most procurement organizations is to reduce the price paid for goods and services. This is the single most important metric used to evaluate

procurement organizational effectiveness. The focus on price to the exclusion of other factors is often detrimental to contract success. The almost obsolete example of this is the razor. Focus on the price of a razor is not a reliable indicator of the true 'cost per shave' of a razor. A vendor could make a sizeable profit by giving away its razor but charging a higher price for the blades. The focus on price obscures the truly important issue of cost.

Other financial concerns

Financial concerns go beyond just price and cost. Cash flow and return is another significant element to be considered. These come into play when clauses relating to payment are negotiated. Managers need to be aware of the many costs that may be incurred before payment from a customer is received. A large contract with unfavorable payment terms can prove disastrous for a supplier who does not have the cash flow to enable ongoing operations.

Liability and indemnity

The question of what should be negotiated is often viewed as unique to a specific transaction or circumstance. To some extent that is true. A company negotiates what it considers important. In addition to price, that generally includes a limitation on liability and indemnification. These relate directly to the amount of risk a company is willing to take in any transaction.

Liability, indemnity, and price have been the top three negotiated terms in the IACCM surveys conducted over the last five years. This demonstrates a consistency in focus on these issues in spite of tremendous change in global commercial markets.

While these issues may be the most frequently negotiated terms there remains considerable discussion on whether these are the terms that most affect the overall success of a contract. Contracting professionals would often argue that time spent negotiating the scope and goals of the contract and the responsibilities of the parties would contribute more to project success than focusing on the concepts of liability and indemnity.

	Terms that are negotiated with greatest frequency	Terms that would be more productive in supporting successful relationships
1	Limitation of Liability	Scope and Goals
2	Indemnification	Entirety of Agreement
3	Price / Charge / Price Changes	Responsibility of the Parties
4	Scope and Goals	Change Management
5	Liquidated Damages	Communications and Reporting
6	Payment	Price / Charge / Price Changes
7	Data Protection / Security	Delivery / Acceptance
8	Intellectual Property	Performance / Guarantees / Undertakings
9	Service Levels and Warranties	Limitation of Liability
10	Warranty	Indemnification
11	Insurance	Payment
12	Responsibilities of the Parties	Service Levels and Warranties
13	Delivery / Acceptance	Audits / Benchmarking
14	Rights of Use	Liquidated Damages
15	Confidential Information / Nondisclosure	Dispute Resolution
16	Dispute Resolution	Data Protection / Security
17	Performance / Guarantees / Undertakings	Assignment / Transfer
18	Invoices / Late Payment	Intellectual Property
19	Change Management	Business Continuity / Disaster Recovery
20	Service Withdrawal or Termination	Information Access and Management

Figure 15.2   IACCM survey of top negotiated terms

Unauthorized or unachievable commitments

A risk that all negotiators must recognize is that of unauthorized or unachievable commitments. Common sense and sound professional judgment are often the best indicators of problems in this area. A supplier who agrees to complete a project in half of the estimated time should raise questions about their understanding of the scope or the resources required. A customer who agrees to an inflated price should raise questions about their ability to pay.

Companies often manage the issue of unauthorized commitments by implementing a formal delegation of authority and approvals. This policy specifies who within the organization is authorized to approve a specific type of contract term. The delegation may be as simple as giving approvals for a level of discount offered or as complex as establishing authority to grant rights in intellectual property. This leads directly to the next practical consideration in negotiation: who negotiates.

15.4 *Who negotiates*

A very practical consideration is deciding who should be involved in the negotiation. If the negotiation is to be done by a single person, is that negotiator knowledgeable of the technical issues, business issues, financial concerns, and legal constraints? If the negotiation is to be handled by a team, a clear leader should be designated.

 Do not forget those who are not at the negotiating table:
- Regulators
- Media
- Shareholders
- The public

There are multiple stakeholders: you need to ensure their interests are protected.

The growth of specialists within large organizations has increased the complexity of many negotiations. It can be the case that gaining internal consensus is harder than the external negotiation. Any variation in standard terms may be the subject of multiple approvals, lengthening the total process. Failure to obtain these approvals can potentially result in the failure to honor a resulting contract term. This can make the entire process far more fragmented and result in minor administrative changes, jeopardizing otherwise profitable business.

While sometimes frustrating, it is important that negotiators do not attempt to take short cuts or exclude specialists. Rather, it should be viewed as part of the negotiation process and the time can be used it to improve arguments. In particular, the experts will rarely have understanding of the needs or interests of the other side and often will not understand the rationale for altered terms or policies. By explaining these to them, and the benefits that will flow to the company, the firm may end up not only with approval, but additionally a more creative, added-value solution.

In practice the overall value of a contract frequently determines who will be involved in the negotiation. More senior professionals will generally negotiate a larger transaction; these negotiators often have considerable flexibility to develop alternatives and approve deviations. More significantly they can often go across functional boundaries, making decisions that impact products, service, delivery, finance or other disciplines.

15.5 *Where to negotiate*

The greatest impact of technology is seen in this area. Business operations have undergone a fundamental shift in the past fifteen years. Negotiation theory was largely developed for face-to-face negotiations. Today most negotiations are conducted in a virtual environment; the globalization of trading relationships and the intervention of networked technologies have fundamentally changed the framework for negotiation. Time zones and distance have in many cases eliminated personal interaction. What was once a face-to-face relationship has moved, in some cases, beyond even telephone or teleconference communication to the simple exchange of documents via email or e-auctions. The concepts of 'positional' and 'principled' negotiation become embedded in the technologies that are selected, and concepts such as the interpretation of body language simply do not exist.

The explosion of communication technology has made one common negotiation tactic obsolete. The unavailability or inaccessibility of management for approval of a contract change is no longer an extremely credible argument. Time pressures and deadlines notwithstanding, all but the most complex or unusual terms that may require specialized analysis, can be reviewed at any level in a timely manner.

As previously mentioned, a major drawback with virtual negotiation is the inability to observe the other side's circumstances. This is especially true when dealing internationally. A negotiator must undertake more active advance research to understand local conditions, the risk of misunderstanding and the possibility of serious misrepresentation. Virtual negotiation carries with it a set of incremental risks that the team should research and take into account throughout the process. Often, a fundamental question that is missed is "What will we do if things go wrong?"

15.6 *How to negotiate*

In the business world the 'how' of negotiation is usually driven by the broader policies and practices of the organization rather than the individual negotiator. If a company operates with a very strong 'powers reserved' approach by specific functions, the negotiation may seem to be a very rigid and fragmented process that is filled with bursts of activity followed by periods of waiting for unseen activity to occur.

A business may dictate how a negotiation will proceed, but it is critical for the individuals involved to have a list of issues that are to be negotiated. Standard forms may be exchanged in a 'battle of the forms', but no progress toward an agreement will be made until those standards are compared and a list of issues to be discussed is developed. A lengthy discussion on the nuances of language is a waste of time if there is no fundamental agreement on how the business will be conducted. There is no short-cut to avoid this step.

Each party must evaluate its approach to the deviations from its standard. Can a deviation be accommodated? What is the financial impact? Is there an operational impact? Are these acceptable? Is there another way that the goal can be accomplished that is more acceptable? Is there a compromise approach?

Going through the entire list of issues in this manner gives everyone a better picture of the deal as a whole. Looking at any single term in a vacuum may give an unbalanced view of a transaction. A single term may be outside the normal risk profile a company desires to maintain, but taken within the context of an otherwise standard transaction it may be perfectly acceptable.

 Wrapping up:

- Ensure a full and mutually agreed record of the agreement
- Establish who is responsible for creating final documents
- Develop materials for the transition / implementation team

Getting agreement is the beginning of the process, not the end

At some point in this evaluation a decision must be made as to whether or not the transaction still makes economic sense given the specifics of the situation. This analysis needs to define the parameters of how far the negotiation can proceed and still achieve the corporate objectives. Once this 'bright line' is established the negotiators can proceed, knowing the boundaries within which they must operate and construct a final solution.

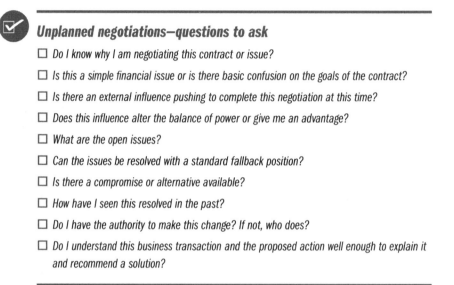

Unplanned negotiations–questions to ask

- ☐ Do I know why I am negotiating this contract or issue?
- ☐ Is this a simple financial issue or is there basic confusion on the goals of the contract?
- ☐ Is there an external influence pushing to complete this negotiation at this time?
- ☐ Does this influence alter the balance of power or give me an advantage?
- ☐ What are the open issues?
- ☐ Can the issues be resolved with a standard fallback position?
- ☐ Is there a compromise or alternative available?
- ☐ How have I seen this resolved in the past?
- ☐ Do I have the authority to make this change? If not, who does?
- ☐ Do I understand this business transaction and the proposed action well enough to explain it and recommend a solution?

15.7 Summary

The ultimate purpose of a negotiation and a contract is to secure a successful output or outcome and to create the framework for a positive business relationship. These lofty goals do not change the fact that much negotiation is done without adequate preparation. Knowing the answers to the fundamental '5 Ws and H' questions enables people to be reasonably prepared for unplanned negotiations.

CHAPTER 16

MANAGE PHASE: TRANSITION TO A NEW CONTRACT

The single biggest problem in communication is the illusion that it has taken place.

George Bernard Shaw

Once negotiations have been successfully concluded and the contract is signed, the Manage phase begins. In some simple contracts, this may be no more than administering the promised delivery. Contract close-out could be almost immediate. This chapter focuses on the growing number of agreements where performance is undertaken over time, where change is frequently endemic and where a sustainable relationship depends on the quality of governance and the delivery of commitments.

It is the Manage phase in the contract management lifecycle that delivers the business outcomes for all parties to the contract. It can affect (positively or negatively) the business opportunities ahead for years to come. Yet, if this phase is so important to business success for buyers and suppliers alike, why do things so often fail to go right? This chapter explores the transition from contract signature to the Manage phase and the critical factors for success.

Top tips:
- Contracts are not perfect—but they set a framework for resolution of those imperfections
- Standard terms and conditions are often ignored—the dangers must be understood
- Plans are not perfect—they must be kept up to date
- The unexpected will happen
- Changes will be necessary
- Claims may arise
- Disputes may occur

16.1 *Culture and attitude*

Culture and attitude have a profound impact on the success or failure of a contract. For example, management at a large international bank was concerned about the disappointing performance of many of its major suppliers. The commitments and promises that were won during the bid and negotiation process often appeared to evaporate in the post-award environment.

A meeting of the senior supplier relationship managers was convened to discuss possible reasons and potential improvements. Mid-way through the meeting, one of those present posed the question: "How

many of you agree that all suppliers are evil?" Every hand was raised in agreement.

In many cases, there is a fundamental lack of trust between suppliers and customers. Implementation and operations teams frequently have a skeptical—or even cynical—view of the other party's honesty, integrity or competence. This is often born out of past experience, but of course such attitudes tend to become self-fulfilling. If we expect poor performance, we are rarely disappointed.

This point about underlying culture and attitudes is of tremendous importance, yet is seldom assessed. The drivers that result in selection of our trading partners are typically more to do with prices, promises, history and senior connections than with cultural fit and organizational alignment. **The factors that were important in winning the contract are in general not the factors that are important in determining its outcome.**

 ### Case study: Poor communication leads to contract breakdown

A US company decided to collaborate with a Japanese partner in developing high-technology products. Their agreement stipulated that the Japanese company would supply the manufacturing, management, and marketing components of the deal, while the American company would supply the technology.

The American representative, who was based in Hong Kong, met with their Japanese counterparts only once every three months to discuss operations. In between these quarterly visits, the two parties communicated in writing and infrequent phone calls.

To the Japanese partner, this periodic (though infrequent) contact signalled that the American partner was not overly committed to the relationship; the Japanese commitment to the partnership began to dwindle as well.

As time progressed, the US company changed strategy to concentrate on a smaller product line; but they never bothered to inform their Japanese partner of the change, nor that they would not receive the technology they had negotiated with the American firm.

The Japanese took a dim view of what they now perceived as an agreement that was signed in 'bad faith'. The relationship soured and ended in arbitration; the outcome was that the partnership was dissolved.

The American firm should have alerted their partner about the change in their strategy, but the Japanese should have communicated their displeasure earlier, rather than allowing it to fester. Poor communication led to losses for both parties.

Loss of trust in a trading partner is significant, and recovery takes substantial effort. Failure to perform, failure to transition the contract, and failure to communicate are often not intentional misdeeds, but careless omissions. These oversights can be prevented by taking action as soon as the contract is signed; joint implementation teams are often useful to plan the initial implementation. There are several important characteristics that can influence success:

- Both parties ensure that the key staff involved with the negotiation participate in the implementation plan. These individuals are responsible for ensuring that the operations teams in both enterprises have a common and consistent view of the contract terms and obligations.
- Both parties work to agree the measurements needed to support committed service levels and key performance indicators.
- They establish formal review procedures and escalation paths for problem resolution.
- Both parties establish a common interface for collection of performance data so that they are operating with a single version of 'the truth' and to enable focus on continuous improvement rather than the allocation of fault or blame.

These fundamental issues of good communications, avoiding blame, commitment to problem solving and appropriate levels of joint working are the types of areas frequently overlooked. In an ideal world, they may be principles that were established in the contract, but often they are not. This does not make the contract irrelevant. Quite the opposite, the contract must provide the foundation for the implementation team and its content must be scrutinized for thorough understanding of rights and obligations that are then embedded into the performance plan.

 Case study: Too many to count

A Managed Services Division represented over 40 percent of corporate revenue yet contributed only 8 percent of profit. Contracts consistently underperformed against expectations and customer satisfaction was some 10 percent below target levels.

The General Counsel (chief legal officer) was tasked with identifying the problem

After some 30 days of research, the General Counsel had identified two major problems. The first was the need to improve the definition of scope, to reduce the frequency of post-award contention and unrecoverable scope-creep.

The second and far bigger challenge was to ensure timely performance of contract obligations. Failures in this area were affecting revenues, cash flow, and anticipated contract extensions. The results included significant payment of liquidated damages and service credits.

The issue was not because of irresponsible or unachievable commitments; it was simply because the myriad of obligations contained in the contract were not being adequately captured, recorded and monitored by the operations team.

On average, when extracted and communicated to every affected stakeholder, each contract had more than 4,000 obligations to be fulfilled. The absence of any standard system or method for contract implementation meant that failures began almost immediately and the operations teams were rapidly overwhelmed by the resulting problems.

Understanding the culture, attitudes and resources of trading partners is not difficult and should come as no surprise. Yet the failure to make this analysis is a common source of disappointing contract results.

- Were they adversarial in the negotiation?
- Did they seek to avoid risk?
- Were they significantly lower in price than their competition?
- Does the company have previous history of dealing with this organization?
- Are there market or media reports about their performance?

There are many ways to gain insight to the likely relationship that lies ahead and no good excuses for the implementation and management team to be unprepared.

Right at the outset, ensure awareness of the precise resources the trading partner is committing:

- What roles do they have?
- What skills or functional background?
- What levels of authority?
- What tools or systems will they be using and how will these interface with those used internally?

Some suppliers may be evil; some customers are incompetent. That does not mean the situation cannot be controlled and delivery successful; but it does require planning and preparation.

16.2 *Understanding the contract*

Integration

The first step in ensuring understanding of the contract is clarity as to which elements constitute 'the contract'. This is becoming steadily more difficult to determine. Driven by a mixture of regulation, diminishing trust and experiences in litigation, the issue known as 'entirety of contract' has risen in importance. This is further affected by the steady move towards more services and solutions contracts, where the agreement may be the only tangible 'product'. Within the agreement, one will generally find a definition of the elements that are formally included, both at the outset and ongoing.

For example, in addition to core terms and conditions of contract, there will typically be formal supplements or appendices, which include documents such as Service Level Agreements (SLA) or Scope / Statement of Work (SOW). There may be product specifications or performance guarantees. In addition, many buyers today insist that all communications associated with the bid are part of the contract, and in the event of dispute there is a possibility that communications within and between the implementation and operations teams are included.

The contract contains many legal terms and there are provisions that will only come into play if things start to go wrong. However, these generally represent a small part of the contract. Most of the agreement comprises clauses and terms that require action, and these must be supported through systems and resources to ensure they are performed.

Anything that is referenced in the agreement as part of the contract is part of the contract. The terminology often seen here is 'incorporated by reference'. This is sometimes done because the contract would be too voluminous if all of the documents were attached. You should begin the clarification process by determining the items specifically included or excluded and ensure it is understood how and when incremental documents formally become part of the contract.

Some typically included documents are SOWs, project plans, specifications, bid and proposal documents, letters of intent, software documentation, or standard terms and conditions. '*Integration*' is the legal operation by which several documents or data sources that are otherwise independent are read together as a single contract. Integration focuses on determining the entirety of a written contract and also determining the order of precedence or priority the different documents should have for contract interpretation.

The challenges of integration have increased with the trend toward reducing the paper exchanges, for example by including references to Internet sites. Combining paper and digital documents is becoming more recognized around the world, but it may ultimately lead to increased administrative costs rather than anticipated savings.

Questions to help determine whether a document, web page or other content is legally part of a contract

☐ Is the document or data identified within the contract, and is the identification specific? For example, is there a version number or copyright date?

☐ Does the contract include the phrase 'incorporated by reference'?

☐ Is there a specific contract clause that states the order of precedence given to documents?

☐ Does the document or data complete the contract in any way?

- ☐ Does the document or data conflict with the contract terms?
- ☐ Is the document or data linked to the contract electronically (via hyperlink) or physically (via staples or binding)?
- ☐ What is the date of the document or data? Can it be placed in sequence before contract signature?
- ☐ What is the source of the document or data?
- ☐ Is the document or data signed by the parties or does it have any other indication of acceptance?
- ☐ Is there anything about the language of the document or data that suggests it was intended to be general marketing material rather than specific contract language?
- ☐ What is the hierarchy of precedence to determine which document or data source applies in the event of a conflict?

With these challenges increasing every day, it is helpful to look for best practice policies. A leading law firm estimates that the average contract for complex services has increased in length by over 50 percent in the last five years. Increased regulation and a tendency by contracting parties to seek to cover all eventualities have resulted in contracts that are both voluminous and hard to use. Unfortunately, their length and the fact that different sections are often prepared by different people increases the probability of contradictions or confusion.

Recognizing this, best practice companies ensure that teams work together to extract the 'metadata' or critical performance requirements from the agreement and, where possible, reconcile differences at the beginning. This may require going back to the original negotiators or project sponsors. It is better to spend time at the beginning of the contract period, ensuring alignment, than allowing issues and difference to emerge at a later time when the results may be more significant or costly.

Contract analysis
After the full extent of the contract is determined, breaking the contract into its essential elements is helpful. This ensures that important information is not buried and overlooked. Contracts can be thought of as having four core elements:

- What is the contract about (scope)?
- Who does what according to the contract (roles and responsibilities)?
- How do we know the contract is working (service levels, measurements, milestones)?
- What happens if something happens or doesn't happen according to the contract (recourse, penalties)?

At this point, it is worth a reminder that the nature of the goods, services or relationship being established by the contract will have significant impact on the extent of analysis and the actions required. For example, a product sale or acquisition may be primarily driven by specification, dates of delivery, unit price, acceptance criteria, warranties and any specific performance criteria. Whether or not these terms are met is generally quite straightforward to determine. A software license is similarly fairly easy to implement, although there will be characteristics that are quite different from those of a piece of equipment (for example, limitations on use, requirements to monitor the number of users, constraints on copying and obligations to implement updates or upgrades). It is in the world of services and solutions that things become more difficult, because acceptability or success is often a matter of judgment and may only be evident after considerable time has elapsed. It is in these circumstances that the contract becomes the operations guide, providing a framework for ongoing performance management.

Scope
As previously mentioned, one of the areas that most commonly causes contention is Scope. This is usually found in an SOW or description of work listed as a section in the main body of the contract or attached as a separate document.

Roles and responsibilities
The second area of critical importance is that of roles and responsibilities. Who has promised to do what, to whom, for whom and when? The roles and responsibilities can be contained in many different places. There are likely to be sections that are specifically titled 'Roles and Responsibilities' but many of the others appear in areas such as the SOW. A summary is essential to individuals not involved in the negotiation process. Individuals entering the commercial transaction at this point have very basic questions, as shown in the checklist.

Checklist: Responsibilities under the contract

☐ *What am I expected to do?*

☐ *Are there specific terms about how I must do it?*

☐ *What are they expected to do?*

☐ *How will I know they have done it?*

☐ *When should things happen?*

Modern contracting methods increasingly facilitate the dissemination of data. For example, electronic contracts may enable specific searches to be undertaken so that a project manager, finance professional or operations executive can immediately extract the areas of contracts relevant to them. Contract management software may be in place, so that central teams undertake the analysis and ensure automated alerts to those responsible for performance.

How do we know the contract is working?
The next area—how we know things are working—is generally driven by performance measurements or (in the case of products or capital projects) formal acceptance criteria. These may take the form of entirely separate signed contracts such as Service Level Agreements that are incorporated into the main contract, or project planning documentation, which may or may not be incorporated, usually as part of the SOW. Agreements that are for high value, or for strategically important products or services, or where scope is complex or uncertain, will typically have milestones or formal 'gateway reviews' at which the parties will determine whether needs and obligations are being met before moving to the next phase of the project. These reviews often lead to significant changes or amendments, sometimes requiring extensive renegotiation.

What happens if the deal goes wrong?
Finally, there will be mechanisms that address what happens if the deal goes wrong. These include the legal provisions related to rights of termination and other things such as indemnities, remedies and *force majeure*. In general, it is not necessary for the implementation team to be familiar with the specifics of these terms since they do not affect day-

to-day operations. However, if there is any hint of a significant disagreement or dispute between the parties, it is essential that expert resources are alerted so that they can advise on the steps to be taken and those to be avoided.

 Case study: Lack of clear understanding proves very costly

Company A contracted with Company D to develop a software system that would enable tracking of high value gems from original mining to eventual sale. It was a complex project because there were multiple stakeholders and no internationally defined process through which the various stages of shipping, evaluation, cutting etc. occurred. In addition, there were major concerns over the security of data due to the potential for hacking and theft. Despite this vagueness, Company A committed to a form and final Scope of Work.

Company D proved less than helpful in assisting Company A with process definition. As a result, Company A experienced major delays and significant cost overruns. However, it did not warn Company D that it could not meet the agreed delivery date until several days before the completed system was due for testing. At that point, it indicated that development of the system would take at least six months more to complete, that the Scope must be revised and that the price would be an additional $2 million. After brief and acrimonious correspondence, Company D issued formal notice of default. Company A responded by giving notice of termination and demanded payment for the work completed to date.

Subsequent litigation resulted in significant costs for Company A, including an award of damages to Company D. By terminating the agreement, Company A had clearly breached its contract and whatever failings there had been on the part of Company D were of no relevance now.

In this instance, the project team at Company A had failed in a number of critical ways:

• On initial review of the contract, they quickly realized that the Scope was challenging and that there were several areas of real uncertainty, resolution of which would depend on close cooperation with Company D. However, they did not alert either their own management or the senior management of Company D about this concern.

- The roles and responsibilities for Company A personnel were relatively clear, but there was no matching clarity over interfaces at Company D. This represented a major risk for performance of the contract, but at no time was it raised with Company D for resolution.
- Performance reviews and milestone meetings were held only sporadically and when they took place, Company A personnel failed to divulge the extent of their challenges. They did highlight a need for more guidance and support from Company D, but when these requests went unanswered there was no escalation.

When it became evident that the project was in major difficulty, the project manager escalated to senior business management. She did not involve staff functions such as Legal or Commercial, but instead made a powerful case to executives regarding the unreasonable behavior of Company D and citing 'repeated requests for support in process definition, which the customer ignored or dismissed as not relevant'. This resulted in the adversarial approach to the customer and an ill-considered notice of termination.

In addition to those provisions there are all sorts of control and reference mechanisms that occur in the contract, such as change management processes or formal notification, which must be understood and followed. There are also very often financial consequences in the event that either party fails to meet its commitments.

Another approach to contract analysis is to identify disparities between the contract terms and conditions that are finally negotiated and the intent at the time of entering into negotiations. This can help realign stakeholder expectations to ensure their views and expectations are reset to reflect the reality of the contract, rather than possibly historic memory of what might have been.

As our various case studies illustrate, a clear understanding of the goals of the contract, the roles and responsibilities, how the performance will be evaluated, and what happens if things do not go as planned will make performing under the contract or managing the contract much simpler. *Every individual responsible for performance should understand these basic elements.*

Interpretation

Contract language varies widely. Some documents are written in very legalistic language using Latin phrases and terms of art found in common law. Other contract documents are written in a plain style that avoids 'legalese'. While some knowledge of legal terminology is required to become fully competent to interpret contracts, the idea that lawyers are the only people who can interpret or understand contracts is unfounded and unwarranted. If ordinary business people are unable to understand a contract, then the contract fails its essential purpose, which is to capture an agreement in writing.

Different legal systems have differing rules that guide interpretation. In the Anglo-American legal tradition, there are specific principles or rules that apply to contract interpretation. In the US the general guidelines or principles for interpretation are:

- **Ordinary meaning**. Language is given its ordinary meaning in a country.
- **Terms of art**. Technical terms and words of art are given their technical meaning. These should be defined in the contract.
- **Interpretation of the whole**. A contract is interpreted as a whole and all of its constituent parts are read as belonging together.
- **Manifest intent**. Conduct of the parties after the contract is signed should determine if the interpretation is reasonable. Where intent is not clearly manifested, interpretation should account for all possible manifestations. The apparent purpose of the contract should be given great weight in determining intent.
- **Specific over general**. Specific provisions qualify general provisions where conflict exists.
- **Construe against drafter**. Interpretation that works against the party who drafted the contract language should be preferred over others.
- **Original language over forms**. Where there is conflict between preprinted contract terms and custom negotiated terms, the negotiated terms take precedence.

Other legal systems may be driven far more by statute—that is, where terms are far more dependent on public policy and in some areas do not allow the parties to negotiate variations, even if both are willing. In many jurisdictions, contract interpretation depends far more on the intent of the parties than it does on the specific words that were used. Hence, in a well-documented Canadian case summarized below, the English-language courts spent considerable time debating the consequences of the positioning of a comma. Their conclusion (which was grammatically correct) was overridden by the French-language courts (to which the losing party was able to appeal) because they focused on an interpretation of intent, which was clearly described in associated non-contractual communications.

 Case study: The devil's in the detail

A tiny typographic error in a sales contract for C-130J Hercules transport aircraft has cost the US aerospace group Lockheed Martin $70 million, according to the Financial Times.

A comma was misplaced by one decimal point in the equation that adjusted the agreed sales price for changes to the inflation rate.

During the contract period inflation was lower than expected, the FT reported, and the customer insisted on the terms of the contract being honored in full.

"That comma cost Lockheed $70 million," Lockheed aeronautics president James Blackwell told the FT.

16.3 Communication

Contract implementation is probably most endangered by poor communication. Sometimes key stakeholders don't even receive a copy of the contract once it is negotiated. At other times it is simply mailed out via email or physical mail with the naïve belief that as long as everybody has a copy, it is going to be properly implemented. Effective and constructive communication eliminates the pitfalls of these two extremes.

 Case study: Confidentiality taken to extremes

A manufacturer and one of its largest customers engaged in lengthy negotiations that resulted in a range of special terms. While the terms were entirely ethical, the manufacturer did not want other customers to know about them. The lawyers therefore agreed a confidentiality clause and the account team were instructed to ensure the terms remained secret.

The contract was to be applied in several countries—but the account team refused to circulate it in order to maintain secrecy. Local subsidiaries were unable to implement the contract: local orders were either delayed, or supplied at the wrong price and under incorrect terms. For the customer, this highlighted the manufacturer's incompetence at contract management and thus how difficult it was to do business together.

Experienced and successful project managers will always advise 'communication, communication, communication'. Communication cannot, however, be confused with information. Communication requires understanding the needs of the recipient and sending simple, targeted messages that explain what needs to be done, why it needs to be done, and the value it brings. It also depends on discipline. Many contracts have multiple stakeholders. When communicating, it is essential that those who need to be advised are copied; it is equally essential that communication is restricted to *only* those who need to know. Too much communication (eg. copying everyone 'just in case') is as bad as too little. In one instance it leads to ignorance, in the other it leads to being ignored.

Everyone has been the recipient of a huge document with an attached message of 'For Your Information'. There is most likely a universal reaction to this form of communication, and it is not likely to be what the sender intended. The communication must be succinct enough that the recipients are reading the things that they really need to know. This is infinitely more effective than confusing them with documentation that has no relevance to the task they are being asked to perform.

The communication process is frequently identified as the key element in successful project implementations. It is essential to bear in mind that a contract may be implemented across multiple cultures. If this is the case, many of the people who are receiving information are not operating in the same native language as the contract. This makes the contract analysis and summary even more critical so that contract terms are expressed in language that others will understand.

 Case study: Compliance requires communication

A multi-national aerospace and defense company operated a policy that required all contract documents to be in English and the Law Department also banned 'interpretation documents' because it feared these would misrepresent the actual terms of the agreement. As a result, communication to the various operating subsidiaries always consisted of an English language contract with no accompanying guidance.

Over time, the company's operations became more international, it undertook increasing volumes of business in emerging markets and intra-company trading also grew in volume. The Corporate Audit function observed considerably more instances of non-compliance with contracts, resulting in both customer and regulatory exposures. Following a policy review, a pilot scheme allowed contracts to be translated into local language and for them to be accompanied by English language contract summaries. Subsequent audits revealed a drop of almost 70 percent in cases of non-compliance.

Specific high-risk or high priority areas should be highlighted to ensure they receive particular attention. These should be communicated positively to encourage cooperation and compliance rather than focusing on consequences of non-performance. With most contracts or projects there will be individuals who, for whatever reason, don't agree with what's being implemented or don't understand why it is being implemented in a particular way. Taking the time and trouble to communicate effectively can mean the difference between success and failure.

 Case study: Managing business risk: "What would the media say?"

Many business risks would be avoided if employees asked a simple question: "If the newspapers were reporting on what I am thinking of doing, what would they say?"

That was the approach one large corporation took to its risk procedures. As a result, they avoided some big mistakes, but they also removed some pointless rules. For example, they were rightly concerned about the potential for bad publicity related to bribery or corruption. But this had led to an inflexible policy where the only permitted customer gifts were a bottle of wine or a bunch of flowers. Clearly, there were circumstances in which neither of these gifts was suitable. The 'What would the media say?' approach proved a far more effective measure of ensuring appropriate judgment by management and allowed a level of empowered decision-making by local staff.

One way to ensure full understanding of obligations and sharing of risks with appropriate stakeholders is to develop a contract-briefing document that summarizes the contract clauses, obligations, actions and rationale behind non- standard areas. This plan identifies who is responsible for doing what and can form the basis of the communication effort. As previously highlighted, in many companies, this communication is increasingly electronic and enabled through contract management software.

There is often a transition meeting held to transfer the knowledge and experience of the individuals who negotiated the contract to the ones responsible for its performance. The contract-briefing document will facilitate that transfer, but—as illustrated earlier in this chapter—it must also be accompanied with some perspective of the challenges faced in reaching the agreement and the status of the relationship between the parties. Knowing the intent of the parties in negotiation can help achieve the original goals of the agreement. Having a contract-briefing document that is jointly prepared by the parties to the contract and holding a joint transition meeting involving both the key negotiators and the implementation team ensures there is one shared view of key contract information. It also has a side benefit that the negotiators jointly explain what they have done and how the contract supports the project implementation.

 Checklist: Essential agenda items for a transition meeting

☐ *Key contract terms and conditions*

☐ *Project deliverables*

☐ *Roles and responsibilities*

☐ *Timescales for delivery and key milestones*

☐ *Project reporting requirements (and who receives reports) and validation that the reports will give early warning of non-compliance or exposures*

☐ *Performance tracking methodology and review meeting structure and participation*

☐ *Budget and payment plans (cash flow forecasts and contingencies)*

☐ *Clarification of aspects of the contract or project requirements*

☐ *How changes will be managed*

☐ *How disputes will be handled*

Moving from set-up to steady-state management may seem like an easy task, but the basics cannot be taken for granted. A well-managed project relies on monitoring performance and handling contractually required activities such as invoicing, payment management, cost recording, participating in reviews or maintaining data and documentation records. While mundane, this work is critically important. It is in this phase that proactive problem identification can occur. Discipline makes a difference between realizing expectations and moving into dispute.

Case study: Informal approach to reviews leads to contract failures

Following a number of high-profile contract failures, a Dutch government agency commissioned research into contract performance management. It discovered that

there was generally an informal hand-over of the contract from its Procurement group to the relevant business unit. Although contracts generally specified performance criteria and embedded the principle of periodic performance reviews, they were less clear about who should organize them or attend. As a result, they occurred only sporadically and then were often conducted as post-mortems and forums to apportion fault. Successful projects were marked by far more disciplined reviews, which operated with formal agendas and focused on identified problems and improvement opportunities.

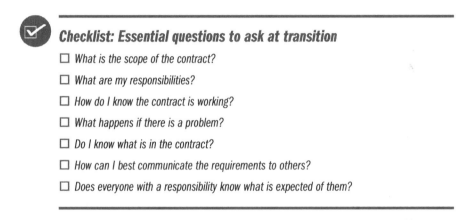

Checklist: Essential questions to ask at transition

☐ What is the scope of the contract?

☐ What are my responsibilities?

☐ How do I know the contract is working?

☐ What happens if there is a problem?

☐ Do I know what is in the contract?

☐ How can I best communicate the requirements to others?

☐ Does everyone with a responsibility know what is expected of them?

16.4 Summary

Positive corporate culture and attitude are important for successfully transitioning a contract from negotiation to performance. An adversarial approach almost guarantees performance problems. The contract must be fully understood by the parties responsible for performance, whether there are a handful of requirements or several thousand. This requires effective communication.

Research shows that before the end of the first third of a project, and as early as one tenth of the way through, project managers can tell with relative accuracy whether it will run as planned or not. It also shows that in many cases, the warning signs are not identified or they are ignored, in the hope they will simply go away.

 __The Manage phase delivers the business outcomes for all parties involved and may affect business opportunities in the future, positively or negatively.__

CHAPTER 17

MANAGE PHASE: MANAGING PERFORMANCE

However beautiful the strategy, you should occasionally look at the results.

Winston Churchill

Once a contract has been effectively transitioned to the individuals responsible for its performance its focus changes yet again. It began as a document to plan performance; now it becomes a tool to manage performance. This book has shown how projects and objectives change through time. The next chapter deals exclusively with managing changes; this chapter focuses on how the contract can be used to ensure both buyers and sellers have received maximum value.

17.1 *Key performance indicators*

Key performance indicators (KPIs) are a type of performance measurement that companies use to gauge their overall success or the success of a particular project. Success may be defined as progress toward a strategic goal or simply repeated achievement of an operational goal. Organizational objectives determine what the KPIs should be. KPIs differ among departments (eg sales, marketing, finance, legal) as well as industry (manufacturing, software, services, education, government). Measurement of KPIs generally requires an assessment of the current business, including the baseline norms and potential process improvement initiatives. This information is frequently organized into a management framework known as a balanced scorecard.

Key performance indicators may be tied to a large project that is comprised of several contracts with multiple companies. The KPIs are then evaluated to judge the progress toward satisfactory and timely completion. These indicators may be spelled out in the contract, or there may be reporting requirements that the buyer then translates into its metrics.

There are several broad categories of indicators. A good KPI is sometimes defined as a SMART indicator. This means that the indicator is specific, measurable, achievable, relevant, and time phased. Beyond this basic guideline, indicators are subdivided into the type of information they reveal. Quantitative indicators are expressed with numbers. Qualitative indicators are those that cannot be presented with a number. Indicators may be used to predict the outcome of a project (a leading indicator) or report on the success or failure of a project after it is completed (lagging indicator).

Evaluating contract performance against the goals as defined in the contract can be difficult, and often proves expensive. Unfortunately the wrong behavior can be incentivized by KPIs when the focus is removed from quality performance and moves to simply satisfying an arbitrary metric. For example, an educational institution that measures only graduation rates might encourage the passing on of inadequately qualified individuals to achieve a goal graduation rate with no thought of the qualification of graduates. A procurement organization that measures only the raw cost of an item purchased does not capture the true cost associated with compromises in quality, delivery, or failures.

17.2 Delivery

Not all valuable measurements are as complex as KPIs. Some are very simple and straightforward. They do not require expensive software systems or elaborate reporting dashboards. Value can be received through the simple comparison of what is actually delivered with what has been contracted.

As indicated in the previous chapters, a contract should very clearly specify what is being purchased and when it will be delivered. For tangible goods this verification process is not complicated. A receiving clerk is usually able to match contents received with a packing slip to confirm receipt. This step is sometimes referred to as inspection and acceptance. The larger and more complex the delivery is, the more rigorous the inspection and acceptance will be.

For a supplier, it is critical to understand exactly what the delivery, inspection, and acceptance requirements stated in the contract are. The common expectation that delivering the product translates into receiving payment can easily break down at this stage. If the buyer has the right to inspect the delivery and then conduct evaluations before accepting and paying for the product the delay can be significant. Reading and understanding the acceptance clause prevents unwanted surprises. It can also help prevent costly errors, such as delivering twelve boxes of products when only twelve individual products were ordered.

As a buyer it is imperative to confirm that both the quality and quantity of the purchased items have been received. Beyond this verification, the buyer needs to make sure that insurance coverage for the products is in place at the appropriate time.

Acceptance may be:
- Partial acceptance
- Complete acceptance with conditions
- Unconditional–complete acceptance

Delivery issues may be more complicated for service contracts. Again, the contract may simply state that services are delivered when performed. This is often found in consulting engagements where resources are provided for an extended period. Sometimes there is a deliverable item that is specified, such as a tax return or audit report from an accountant. Other contracts may track delivery in terms of milestones that are completed. In each of these cases it is critical to evaluate whether or not the contract is moving toward a successful completion, and monitoring deliveries is one way to verify progress.

Delivery questions
- ☐ Has the correct product been delivered?
- ☐ Is the quantity correct?
- ☐ Did the proper party pay delivery or customs fees?
- ☐ Has the full order been fulfilled?
- ☐ Is insurance in place to protect the property?
- ☐ What inspection needs to be carried out to ensure that quality and performance standards have been achieved?
- ☐ Have the items been delivered when promised?
- ☐ Are there milestones or interim deliveries? Is the contract moving toward successful completion?

17.3 *Invoicing*

The activity that usually follows delivery and acceptance is invoicing. The guideline that there should be adequate clarity in the contract regarding pricing is evaluated in this step. In actual performance, it is critical not only to deliver the correct item, but also to generate an appropriate invoice.

The contract should clearly specify the cost for the goods and services as well as the units of measure. This should correspond to the invoices. Any delivery charges, taxes, or fees imposed for import/export should also be detailed and match the contract. For a delivery that is complete, the charges should match the contract total. Interim deliveries should correspond to the level of contract completion. Contracts that have extended periods of performance may allow for price escalation. If an invoice is found to have increased prices, it should be verified to confirm that the increase is allowable.

If invoice timing is addressed in the contract, it should be followed during the performance of the contract. Contracts may specify how often a supplier may bill (weekly, semi-monthly, monthly, annually, upon performance, etc.) Invoices should match the contract terms, and buyers should verify that each item has been billed only once.

We have briefly mentioned ERP systems before. Many companies use these systems to automate accounting functions. In these cases global price increases may be implemented and applied to all invoices. If specific invoicing terms have been negotiated it may be necessary to raise the issue with the supplier.

 Invoicing questions

☐ *Is the unit of measure clear (hours, boxes, weights, etc)?*

☐ *Does the price per unit match the contract?*

☐ *Are delivery charges itemized and charges as promised in the contract?*

☐ *Have all taxes and duties or fees been accounted for?*

☐ What is the time period covered by the invoice?

☐ How frequently are invoices generated?

☐ If any surcharges have been added to the invoice (environmental fees, fuel surcharges, etc.) are they allowed by the contract?

17.4 Benchmarking pricing

Pricing is the focus of many negotiations. Beyond any original discount, many contracts include special terms for future transactions. Volume purchase agreements are common. In this arrangement a customer may receive a larger discount or other incentive after a cumulative purchase threshold is met. Both sides must be attentive to these types of agreements. For suppliers it indicates that the customer is satisfied with the product or service, and acknowledging customer loyalty can be a positive and ultimately profitable endeavor. For the buyer, it is an opportunity to leverage further purchases to include options such as free delivery, additional discounts, or priority fulfillment.

Some contracts expand beyond the original scope because the buyer has been extremely pleased or because there is a greater demand. When a buyer recognizes that this has happened, it may be worthwhile to open discussions with the supplier to see if the increased spending translates into any other benefits.

Rapid changes in the marketplace means that pricing can change dramatically in a short period of time. A fantastic price on an item that is negotiated in January may not be quite as spectacular in October. Buyers and sellers must continually benchmark pricing against the larger marketplace to make sure that their contracts continue to deliver good value.

Pricing questions

☐ Is the price charged the price that was negotiated?

☐ Has the price changed either up or down?

FUNDAMENTALS OF CONTRACT AND COMMERCIAL MANAGEMENT

☐ If the price has changed, is that change in accordance with the contract terms?

☐ Is it time to discuss pricing with the supplier again due to changes in the market or the quantities purchased?

☐ What is the price for the goods or service in the market today?

☐ Am I leveraging this contract to receive the best value from it, whether I am the buyer or seller?

17.5 Contract targets and other measurements

In an ideal world, the original business case for the contract would clearly state the desired business outcome from the resulting agreement, and those objectives would translate to measurable targets. Unfortunately this is not often the case in the real world. Without clearly articulated outcomes, it is difficult—if not impossible—to evaluate the success of the arrangement. Contract targets and other measurements help to put an objective perspective on the subjective question: "How is the contract going?"

Targets differ between buyers and sellers. For the purchaser, many contracts will have a savings target. This may be monetary savings (for example, compared with the cost of the previous contract) or non-monetary, such as through more efficient processes. The targets may also be for increased quality or better performance. For a supplier, the contract many have a target for profit margin, sales volume or turnover.

Targets may evolve if the contract is for a substantial period of time. As both parties benefit from good performance they should also be continually challenged to improve, whether it is through better delivery, higher margins, or lower costs. It should not be the case that the only improvements in performance are seen when there is a requirement to rebid!

Benchmarking and auditing are two essential tools used by buyers to measure the quality of a transaction. These tools are complementary, and using both methods together can be more beneficial than using a single technique.

Benchmarking, which is simply comparing costs with other parties, is helpful where there are similar services being provided to similar organizations under similar conditions. This ideal situation seldom, if ever, exists—and if it did, commercial confidentiality would probably preclude any contract disclosure to a third party. However, for many goods or services where there is a repeatable deliverable, where there are hourly or daily charges for skill types (eg staffing or professional services contracts), for utility, insurance or financial services, benchmarks are quite common. Internet searches can be used to obtain public data easily.

Regular auditing is essential for buyers. Verifying that goods are delivered to the right quality specifications and according to the prices quoted in the contract is a fundamental protection. Some contracts may promote auditing through open-book arrangements where costs are transparent between the contracting parties.

Sellers also benefit from benchmarking and auditing. The same public data available to buyers is also there for sellers to review. This enables them to validate their pricing and also to better understand the current marketplace and their place within it. Audits are a basic key for sellers to continually ensure that they are delivering according to the contract and are being paid in accordance with its terms.

17.6 *Regular management of the contract*

There is nothing routine about the regular management of a contract. The day-to-day management of the contract should be planned at an early stage and formally assigned to someone. If there is no contract manager, someone needs to become responsible for the ongoing oversight of the project. This can be facilitated with regular meetings between the suppliers and the purchaser, perhaps involving key stakeholders from either party or at least involving their input.

These meetings can answer the question "How is the contract going?" by reviewing the performance of services, often through the key performance indicators or service levels, or against the targets set as discussed above. The meeting should also look at the payments, which are often a cause

for dispute—are they as expected? Are the profits (seller) or savings (buyer) being realized?

Resolving complaints is another common agenda item. Either party may have raised issues. A goal of these meetings should be to ensure that solutions are found to complaints and they are not simply pushed to one side. For the buyer it is important to have some way of understanding the level of satisfaction of the end users of the product or service. This may be done informally or through surveys if there are many users scattered across the globe.

These meetings should also be a forum for other stakeholders to be involved in the management of the contract—finance, legal, users, procurement or technical personnel may all want to participate at some point. It is critical that at all parts of an organization that interface with a contract come together to make certain that any changes, innovative approaches or solutions are clearly communicated.

The day-to-day meetings should also be a way of managing risks. Risks should be flagged and counter-measures or risk mitigation strategies identified and implemented. Lessons should be learned and documented, to ensure that improvements are put in place and mistakes are not repeated.

 ### Documenting and sharing lessons learned:

- Sharing and consolidation of experience
- Identify patterns
- Repeat success, avoid failure
- On-going reference source
- Develop and display personal and team expertise

If companies use contract managers, they are specialists at managing this relationship and evaluating performance. Contract managers are most valuable when they are the key interface with the supplier or the customer. The contract manager is enabled by the rest of the team to perform this task by knowing intimately all details about the contract—the performance, the expenditure, any changes being undertaken or complaints outstanding. This approach leads to better project results for all parties.

17.7 *Summary*

Very few companies undertake a rigorous review of actual performance after the contract is signed. In order to be effective, there must be a basic review of the critical pricing, delivery, and invoice contract terms. These terms should be compared with goods and services delivered and received; this is the most fundamental level of contract management.

Beyond these basics, many contract elements can prove useful as key performance indicators to evaluate company performance trends. On large value contracts and projects a similar system can be used on the overall program. The nature of the project determines the level of effort expended in drafting and negotiating the contract; in the same way it should also guide the effort spent in its evaluation. A complex evaluation system is probably not worthwhile for routine commodities, but is essential for large and strategic construction or IT projects. This oversight can be helpful to ensure a successful outcome.

A contract must be managed for both sides to receive the expected value from the transaction.

CHAPTER 18

MANAGE PHASE: MANAGING CHANGES AND DISPUTES

The only thing permanent is change.

Heraclitus

Everyone is conscious of the speed of external change. New technologies, new regulations, new competitors or suppliers, new markets, new products or services, new economic conditions—these are just some examples of the volatile environment in which we operate.

Change is not intrinsically good or bad. Change is a fact of life. If contracts are going to reflect business realities then they must be able to change as business changes. Historically this has been done with many lawyers, extensive document exchanges, and physical signatures. Project and operations teams increasingly operate through social media, such as Instant Messenger and effective change management must embrace these new technologies if it is to deliver business results.

Change is endemic and always will be. Companies and business do not stand still. If managed properly, change can be a significant opportunity to alter or improve a service delivered through a contract.

The average contract now has 40 percent more amendments during its lifetime than it did five years ago. This chapter explores the pervasiveness of change in organizations today; the impact of change on contracts and their management; and processes for managing change effectively. Unfortunately even good change management will not entirely prevent disputes from occurring. The chapter will conclude with a look at the dispute process.

18.1 *The pervasiveness of change*

It is not surprising that the failure of contract procedures to keep pace is causing issues. Disagreements over change management are among the top causes of claims and disputes between trading partners. Often the problem only becomes evident some time later—perhaps at the point of acceptance or following a user satisfaction review. The speed of change often means that:

- Contract changes are not properly recorded
- Contract records are not properly maintained
- Key stakeholders are not advised of changes.

Any one of these failures threatens performance—when combined they deliver disaster.

Change introduces other issues and challenges. For example, it is often the source of disagreement over scope or functionality. Customers naturally want changes included at no extra charge; suppliers take the opposite perspective, especially if they experienced tough price negotiations.

There is a commonly held view in business that a contract should address every eventuality and document a clear, black and white, unchanging picture of the commercial relationship. Consequently change is often viewed as a problem and a failure. Experienced business people realize, however, that change is not about failure. In any complex situation or where a project extends over a long period of time, change is inevitable. Static conditions are very rare and may even indicate hidden risks.

Recognizing change

When the contract is negotiated and signed, the final contract documentation represents the agreed position between the parties. *Any alterations, enhancements, deletions or substitutions are, therefore, changes.*

In many cases a contract will specify the process to be followed to initiate and document changes. A comprehensive understanding of the basic obligations and requirements will enable managers to recognize changes as they occur during the project.

Change management requires many of the skills and tactics of the original negotiation, with each side having different goals and objectives. For example, there may be concerns around financial consequences, timing or the possibility of trade-offs.

Factors of change

The major factors of change can be categorized as follows:

- Changing business needs—particularly prevalent in a medium to long-term contract.

- Changing organization—the customer and/or supplier undergoes some form of restructuring whether due to merger, acquisition, new location or new products.
- Technology shifts—technology develops continuously and it may be appropriate to leverage a particular development
- Organizational priorities change—the customer may consider other projects as being higher priority affecting key personnel, the money available or the timing
- New legislation or regulation—unavoidable external requirements over which no party to the contract has control
- Imperfect scope description—elements of the project's design and deliverables do not fully meet the defined need and require re-working.
- New regulations—may require changes to form or function (e.g. to meet health and safety rules) or nature of responsibilities (e.g. data protection and privacy).

While change generally falls into one of these categories, there are underlying causes for contract changes. There may be errors or omissions in the contract documents. No matter how much thought is put into preparing scopes of work, no effort is immune from clerical or transcription errors. This is even more likely to happen when a number of versions of contract documents are exchanged. As the complexity of the transaction increases there is more chance for error.

But complexity also means that many changes are inevitable and could not reasonably have been forecast. Sometimes—for example where the parties are attempting to be innovative—it may be impossible to be precise about the scope and output at the time of contract signature. Ideally, the contract form in these situations is designed to enable flexibility.

 Case study: Innovative results require innovative contracts

Background
Company M wanted to build a new application that would improve communications and record retention with its dealer and distributor network. Development was urgent because the application was seen as offering a way to meet new regulatory

requirements. The internal IT group quickly recognized that it lacked the resources needed to undertake the development and therefore decided to outsource the work to a major Indian provider, Company I. Due to uncertainty over precise requirements, the IT group and the developers agreed that the best way forward would be through an 'agile development'. This meant that they would form a joint working group, with a small number of Company M personnel working on-site at Company I and vice-versa.

The contract
The legal team at Company M saw the agreement in different terms. Their conversations with senior management led them to a traditional time and materials contract, where time was of the essence. It did not include significant milestone reviews, which would be typical of an 'agile' contract because they are used to capture progress to date and reset the scope and goals based on increasing understanding of requirements.

Company I had limited experience of contract negotiation and management, since culturally contracts were seen more as an administrative requirement than as a management tool. The contract was therefore signed with minimal amendment.

The project
After several months, management at Company M became concerned over the apparent lack of progress. While the IT department was issuing reassuring reports and was working harmoniously with the developer, the testing and availability dates remained unclear. Executives at Company I were shocked when they received a legal letter reminding them that time was of the essence and that they must meet the contractual obligation or face severe consequences. They were further advised that Company M wanted firm assurances within seven days that the full deliverable would be available on the committed date; without this assurance, Company M would place the work with a competitive developer and seek recompense from Company I.

The result
The project did not progress smoothly and ended up in litigation in the London courts.

The underlying issues
There were clear failings in this situation that illustrate many of the areas we have discussed.

- Poor communications within Company M led to confused expectations and a misdirected supplier.
- Company I's immaturity in contracting was not recognized and its own management had not appreciated the very real differences in contracting culture between India and Western Europe.
- The implementation teams set their own agenda and working methods without reference to the contract terms.
- Company M, in developing the contract, had not established the types of reviews and change procedures necessary for such a high risk and high importance project.
- The project manager from Company M had failed to appreciate the fundamental risks of the project and to take the commercial steps needed to protect against them. Not surprisingly, that failure proved extremely career damaging.

Impact of change

A contract change generally has one or more of the following major impacts:

- Cost. The contract price may increase, decrease or remain unchanged. The change may, however affect the cost base of one or both parties to the contract either directly or indirectly.
- Program duration. This could decrease, or increase or remain unchanged.
- Supplier performance or quality. This could improve or deteriorate. Key performance indicators (KPIs) or functionality and the results of monitoring the supplier performance to them may change. New KPIs or specifications may need to be established.
- Service Level Agreements (SLAs). These may not be met or could be altered to reflect changing customer requirements, so new SLAs may need to be established.
- Statement of Work (SOW). The SOW may need to be adjusted in terms of responsibilities, deliverables or milestones. If something happens that causes one of the parties to have to perform more work than originally planned or included in the original price structure, this would create a change to the scope of work that can be charged.

Even if it is agreed that a change has no visible effect on the contract terms it should still be recorded in accordance with the process; otherwise it might become a later source of dispute, or internal exposure—for example in an audit or executive review. These 'no impact' changes, when taken individually, may have no quantifiable impact, but taken in total they may actually accumulate to have a significant impact. Review this type of change periodically to ensure the project is not suffering cumulative effects.

18.2 *Initiating and documenting change*

Some contracts restrict the ability to initiate change requests. More generally change requests may come from either side. The customer, the supplier, or both, can request a contract change. It is important to understand who within both the customer's organization and the supplier's organization can initiate contract change or accept a contract change. If it is unclear who can initiate a change or accept a change then project control and accountability are jeopardized.

12 general rules for negotiating change:

1. Never lose control of your emotions; avoid allocations of blame
2. Be confident—never look scared or worried
3. If a deal looks too good to be true, it probably is
4. A price is too high only if the buyer thinks it's too high
5. To counter negotiation tactics, you must first recognize them
6. Do not give out more information than is needed
7. Keep focused—remember the big picture
8. Your first offer sets a tone for the negotiations
9. Make concessions carefully
10. Do not be too predictable
11. Negotiation success is 80% preparation and 20% tactics during negotiation
12. Know when to take the deal, know when to walk away, and know when to run!

The contract should define what form change requests should take, where they should be sent, the process and authority by which they are reviewed and accepted or rejected, and the form that communication of the decision will take.

The process and authorities will vary depending on the scope and consequences of the change. It is important to have these parameters clearly defined and communicated in both parties' organizations. This procedure is called a **change control** procedure.

 Case study: Managing cumulative changes

Jim and Alice were project managers, overseeing work on a new power station. As the project progressed and they became more familiar with each other's working style, they increasingly communicated using instant messaging on their smartphones. This was far faster and more convenient, especially since much of their time was on-site and without direct access to their company email system. Over time, these communications even came to include minor changes to the project—slight amendments to design, altered dates or sequences for deliverables. It was their mutual intent to record these changes formally, but workload was heavy and 'getting things done' to meet the due date was their priority. As a result, many of the amendments they had agreed went unrecorded.

When the project overran by more than 30 days, Jim's company faced a liquidated damages claim from the customer and sought to pass this to Alice's company as the main sub-contractor. Alice's company rejected much of the claim, on the basis that 20 days of delay had been agreed by Jim through cumulative changes. They listed these based on notes maintained by Alice; Jim had no equivalent record, but could not deny that there had been an 'informal' change process operating through their instant messaging. However, Jim's company pointed to the formal change process contained in the contract and rejected Alice's log since it was not compliant with this procedure.

At final acceptance of the completed work, Jim's company noticed several items that were not in compliance with customer requirements. They therefore demanded that Alice's company should rectify these errors and omissions immediately and at no charge. Not surprisingly, Alice's company rejected this demand on the basis that they had met the original specification and that the variations requested were not covered by appropriately agreed change orders.

There was of course an eventual agreed compromise between these companies, but failure to follow procedure had led to considerable wasted time and potential damage

to the relationship. The good news is that it led to a review of change procedures at both companies, which resulted in streamlining their approach and new equipment for the project managers!

Change control process

Changes may be managed differently as the project moves through its lifecycle. The procedure should be as simple as possible to be effective. It should identify the stages through which a requested change passes.

The change control process should be easy: easy to find, easy to access and easy to monitor. There should consistency and compatibility within the entire project team. For example, use the same data, terminology and electronic interchange to facilitate communication and compliance.

Change control form

A very effective project management tool is to have a standard change control form. Optimally the form and process are placed online where people can access and review them. Monitoring the progress of any proposed changes allows them to be dealt with promptly before they become urgent.

A typical change control form is simple and short, including the key stages of change management:

- Identification of proposed change
- Evaluation of proposed change
- Approval or rejection of change
- Implementation of approved change
- Verification of compliance with the approved change

Note that the phrase 'Proposed change' is used. Until the change is actually approved and implemented with a formal contract modification, it is not a change.

It is important that changes to a contract are communicated as widely as the original contract was communicated. If there are parallel projects the appropriate managers should be informed of any changes as well. No one likes surprises!

Accepting a change

The decision whether to accept or reject a change should be based on an analysis of the situation. Evaluation of the change should be based on the complexity of the contract and the criticality of the change. The fundamental business logic should consider the following factors:

- Is the change unavoidable (e.g. legislative changes, mergers, etc)?
- Does the change increase the overall benefit to the organization (taking into account any impact on the costs, benefits, timescales and risks)?
- Is the project team able to make such a change?
- Is the change best done now, or would it be more beneficial to defer it until the current work is complete?

18.3 *Contract claims*

Small scale contract claims often arise when there are problems with the change control process or disagreement regarding a proposal's acceptance. The supplier can initiate a claim for a variety of reasons: the customer's failure to meet responsibilities, having to do more

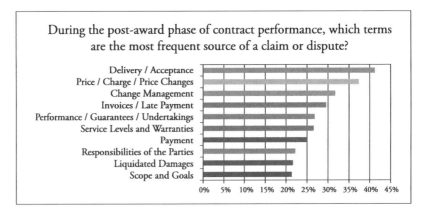

Figure 18.1   Major causes of dispute and claims

work than agreed, incurring additional cost or having the program changed by the customer outside the formal change control process. Similarly, the customer may initiate a claim if contract conditions have not been met.

With good change control procedures, followed by both parties, claims should be minimized. However, they might occur if:

- Procedures were not followed
- A change was rejected
- A supplier carries out 'unauthorized work' such as may be asked for or instructed by someone who does not have the authority to request it
- The supplier raises an issue, which is not dealt with under the change control process
- Either the customer or supplier loses trust in the other party
- The project is moving towards a dispute.

 Claims should be seen as a red flag that all is not well.

 Case study: Performance impact of complex change processes

A multi-national oil and gas company had delegated contract management responsibility to the individual business and product divisions. Project managers and engineers typically oversaw performance. In the event of a claim or dispute, they were required to involve central staff. This resulted in a lengthy resolution process and unpredictable additional work.

Not surprisingly, the project managers and engineers sought to avoid claims and disputes—typically by either accepting supplier requests or ignoring supplier shortfalls. Cumulatively, this had substantial impact on the company's performance—especially since the message to suppliers was that delays and cost overruns were acceptable.

In this case, a culture of claim and dispute avoidance led to a lack of data and therefore no ability to drive improvements in the contract management process. Independent estimates put the cost of this process failure at almost 12 percent of annual revenue.

In some cases the claims process can be a function of the prevailing business culture. It can be ingrained in an industry, part of the norm in a country or a pattern of behavior with a particular customer or supplier, clawing back concessions made during the contract negotiations. For example, in civil engineering claims have been an inherent part of the project management process. Suppliers frequently try to raise a claim, often with the intent of increasing the contract price. Claims may be presented at the end of a contract in an attempt to increase costs. Claims can form a very significant part of the project price. Unfortunately, claims almost always damage the business relationship

Sometimes it may not be wise to manage a claim through the change process. It may be more appropriate for a claim to be handled separately from contract performance through a more formalized dispute process.

18.4 *Contract disputes*

A dispute can be defined as an unresolved issue between contracting parties.

In many instances, a dispute occurs because the parties have different perceptions, inferences or beliefs in relation to the facts and circumstances. Parties may view contractual entitlements and respective values as fundamental rights or obligations. When contractual provisions are unclear or ambiguous, the differences in the perspectives create 'interpretations' which in turn can cause the parties to shift from a harmonious relationship to one in dispute. In some cases the parties may not even realize or agree that they are in fact in dispute.

The nature of the dispute may also reflect the complexity of the project or its profile or value to one or all parties or the significance, frequently financial, of the matter in dispute.

18.5 *The causes of disputes*

The causes of disputes change with every contract and set of circumstances. In simple terms, the four underpinning causes of contractual dispute are:

- Ill-will between the contracting parties
- Miscommunication, including incomplete or misdirected communication, poorly made or maintained contractual documentation, or inadequacies present from the initial source selection process
- Changes in market conditions, causing one party to seek a way out from its commitments
- Departure from agreed or reasonable processes, procedures or standards, in contract or at law

 ### Case study: The critical omission

ABC Engines entered into an agreement with XYZ Aerospace to develop a new type of engine for a fleet of aircraft. ABC felt confident in finalizing the contract with their counterparts from XYZ. All the arrangements for protecting ABC's upfront investment seemed to be watertight. In the event of significant volume shortfall, or if the program was terminated for any reason XYZ would be liable to reimburse all direct costs plus a nominal margin.

The investment needed to develop the new engine was estimated to be $365 million. XYZ had agreed an up-front contribution of $20 million and a further lump-sum of $30 million upon successful testing of the prototype. Further revenues would come once the engine was in production; XYZ had provisional advance orders for nearly 100 aircraft.

Upon signature, XYZ paid the $20 million it had agreed. Development progressed well and the prototype test was ready to be scheduled. However, before it could take place, XYZ issued a notice of delay, under Clause 18.4 of the contract.

Staff at ABC were dismayed to find that their contract did not specify how long the period of delay could be. After several months, it became obvious that XYZ had no intention of proceeding with the project, but was not announcing formal termination so that it would avoid its liabilities under the contract.

At this point, ABC had invested almost $180 million. A poorly drafted clause, not properly linked to the termination provisions, had proven an extremely costly mistake.

While this particular case study illustrates the importance of thoroughly reviewing termination rights and consequences, others have provided examples of miscommunication and the failure to follow procedures.

It is easy to state that the main cause of contractual dispute is money because it is the most common subject. Customer personnel need and want the project and contract deliverables at the agreed price within the agreed time and to the agreed level of quality. The supplier needs and wants to be paid the contractual value, which in turn delivers a return to the supplier's shareholders. A perceived, inferred, believed or known departure or deviation from the financial expectations of the customer or the supplier can result in escalation to a dispute as well as influence its intensity and magnitude.

Contracts are first and foremost economic instruments. Unfortunately they may become a vehicle for 'last resort' protection of assets. In this position, regardless of the outcome of the resolution process, there are no 'winners'. Both parties have spent enormous amounts of money, time, and resources to achieve a victory—and both have lost.

18.6 *Resolving common operational disputes*

Money and contractual performance

To prevent or resolve money-related disputes, effective and efficient project management is of prime importance. This requires the collection and review of appropriate project performance data. This management will facilitate the recognition of potential problems and will also provide a factual basis to refute inaccurate claims. Proving whether or not the contractual performance requirements have been met is fundamental to resolving deviations or changes before they escalate into disputes.

Information

Information is another aspect that can frequently lead parties into a dispute. The contract may or may not specify exactly what data the supplier is required to provide and when. Customers, however, will expect comprehensive, robust information from the supplier, which meets the requirements as they see them. This disparity in expectations

can lead to dispute. The contracting parties rightfully expect accurate and useful information to flow between them in a timely manner.

For example, if one party requests extra information or detail, the other party may object, on the basis of the additional systems and manpower to prepare and present the data. To avoid this potential dispute, data requirements should be detailed during contract negotiation. This should include any data required for the efficient processing of invoices.

People

Dealing with people always creates issues. No project should fail or be delayed because of incompetent or difficult individuals. Personality clashes, however, must be distinguished from issues of performance.

There are often contract provisions regarding the appointment of personnel, as some provisions require the parties to approve appointees and their skill sets before an individual takes up a position. A clear structured approach to relationships between the parties at all levels can also minimize the possibility that the dispute is personality-based.

18.7 *The contract and dispute resolution*

If the contract specifies a mechanism for dispute recognition, management and resolution, then the parties are obliged to follow that process before seeking resolution outside the contract.

Where the contract does not expressly provide for dispute handling and resolution the parties need to reach some consensus in relation to handling and resolution of disputes. This is somewhat problematic if the parties are already in dispute. In such cases the dispute handling and resolution process or mechanism may be decided by others, either by managers not involved on a day-to-day basis or by taking legal action. This usually does not produce an outcome that is desired by either party.

If the contract is silent on the method for resolving disputes, there will generally be a three-step escalation through the business. This will generally follow a course of:

- Use management skills to resolve the dispute at the operational level and within the general requirements of the contract between the parties without external advice or assistance
- Escalation to senior management or an outside source such as a mediator to facilitate a resolution
- Let the legal system resolve the dispute.

The costs of the resolution process rise as it progresses through the process. The relationship between the parties is also damaged the longer a dispute continues and the more formal its resolution becomes. The farther a dispute progresses, the less likely it becomes that either party will be satisfied with the outcome. This may include significant damage to wider market reputation—either in terms of reliability as a supplier, or trustworthiness as a business partner.

18.8 Consequences of disputes

A recent study from the Centre for Effective Dispute Resolution (CEDR) identified that conflict costs UK businesses around £33 billion a year. This was directly due to poor conflict management. The key conclusions identified in the study confirm that 80 percent of disputes have a significant impact on the smooth running of business, and that managers may spend over 689 days of time trying to sort out any cases valued in excess of £1 million.

This is a distraction that may prove too expensive to sustain over time, as it is time taken away from revenue or value-creating tasks. In contrast, in-house teams spent on average 172 days on similarly valued cases that were resolved without involving outside parties.

18.9 Avoiding a dispute

The best way to avoid disputes is to define the project well at the outset, develop an appropriate contract, and then manage those contracts and projects effectively. It is recommended from time to time to undertake a risks audit, reviewing the contracts and projects that are ongoing to ensure that lessons have been learned from past mistakes.

The change process must be managed to identify potential disputes. Lawsuits do not spring into being without precursors. Communication between the parties at all levels of the project team enables managers to deal with issues as they arise. When red flags pop up, such as non-payment or non-performance, they should be addressed immediately. It may simply be an oversight, or it may be an indicator of a more significant problem.

Resolving issues at the operational level provides the best opportunity for a cost-effective solution.

18.10 *The formal dispute resolution process*

It is not uncommon for a contract to specify that a full dispute resolution process occur in the event of a conflict. This would entail some or all of the following steps:

Negotiation—The parties participate in a negotiation to determine the root cause of the issues and the losses involved to decide a sustainable outcome based on the interests of both parties.

If unsuccessful in negotiation then the parties progress to mediation.

Mediation—The parties use a third party neutral mediator to guide them through a structured process to determine the most sustainable outcome in the interests of the parties and enabling the parties to decide the most appropriate future for their business relationship. Sometimes this approach may be embedded in the entire contracting process.

For example, the US construction industry used to be notorious for its high levels of contention and litigation. Some years ago, it became a common approach to appoint a 'wise intermediary'—someone familiar with the industry and respected by both parties. For a small fee, shared between the parties, this individual familiarizes him or herself with the contract and is available to advise if the parties cannot reach agreement at any phase of contract execution. While that advice is non-binding, the evidence suggests it is normally accepted—some estimates suggest almost 90 percent of the time.

If unsuccessful in non-binding mediation then the parties progress to arbitration.

Arbitration—The parties use a third party neutral arbitrator or team of arbitrators to hear the positions in an agreed forum, such that an award may be determined by the arbitrator after reasoned deliberation in accordance with the common law and the rules of natural justice. Depending on the terms of the contract and the applicable legal system the arbitral decision may be final and binding or subject to possible subsequent litigation.

If unsuccessful in non-binding arbitration, the parties then progress to litigation.

Litigation—The parties use a court of competent jurisdiction to hear the evidence in an adversarial manner in accordance with the doctrine of precedent and the rules of natural justice, to hand down a final and binding determination, notwithstanding any rights to appeal.

There is much debate over whether arbitration is cheaper or more expensive than litigation. Indeed, a growing number of courts today expect that the parties will have first attempted mediation or arbitration and punishes those who refuse to seek resolution this way. But regardless of what method is pursued, disputes are expensive and the total in terms of money and man-hours is costly to both parties regardless of who is the ultimate winner.

The bottom line is to avoid disputes if at all possible, or resolve them as efficiently and effectively as possible. That is why, in percentage terms, disputes are rare—and why ultimately the quality of contract management is far more important than the contract document itself.

 ### Change control and dispute resolution questions to ask

☐ Is this change the result of an error or omission in the original contract?

☐ Is the change going to increase or decrease the price of the contract?

☐ Is the program duration changed?

☐ Will the quality of the project deliverable be affected?

- [ ] *Is the service level changed?*
- [ ] *Is the scope of work increased or decreased?*
- [ ] *Who needs to initiate contract change?*
- [ ] *Who needs to approve a change?*
- [ ] *What is the change control procedure?*
- [ ] *Does the process use the available technology?*
- [ ] *Is the change control form easy to use?*
- [ ] *Is there a history of claims with this trading partner?*
- [ ] *Is there a dispute process specified in the contract?*
- [ ] *How can I reduce the chance of a claim or dispute?*

18.11 Summary

Change is part of life and part of business. It is neither good nor bad, but it must be managed effectively if it is to have a positive business result. A good change management process is simple to use and readily accessible; it takes advantage of the technology that the project and operational teams already use. This does not mean that the parties avoid a formal approval process that is necessary for accountability and control, but this process is as streamlined as possible.

Changes that are not formally agreed often move to contract claims, which are usually resolved through a more detailed process that involves escalation through management on both sides. Contract claims may still be successfully resolved in a timely manner, but they frequently raise red flags that the management on both sides should review the project and contract.

Failure to resolve claims may move the issue into the realm of a formal dispute. This should be avoided if at all possible. Disputes are expensive and generally damage the business relationship beyond repair.

Changes do not need to result in disputes. The goal is proactive and effective management that yields a positive result for both parties.

CHAPTER 19

CONCLUSION: PUTTING THE PIECES TOGETHER

It's easy to make a buck. It's a lot tougher to make a difference.

Tom Brokaw

At the start of this book we asked: "Why do I need to know anything about contracts?"

Quite simply, contracts are the language of business. Contracts are a straightforward means to organize the important information for a transaction. Contracts provide a framework or context to ensure that the right questions are being asked, answered and documented.

It may not have been Einstein who developed the formula that **time = money**, but it is certainly an accepted law of business. Understanding the transaction process and effectively using contracts brings efficiency to the way we do business.

19.1 Asking questions

This book is filled with information and guidelines, but it is also packed with questions. Those questions may be the most significant portion of the book. This text only comes alive when you follow the process and go through those questions, personalizing them for the project you are working on today.

The ability to ask questions effectively is important for any career. This questioning needs to move beyond gathering facts to exploring the thought process and assumptions of colleagues and project teams. Identifying how and why teams are moving in a particular direction could avoid many simple misunderstandings that plague contracts and projects.

Questioning projects must be done in a positive light and with the goal of solving or preventing problems. Too often individuals ask questions with a very different agenda in mind. It makes everyone uncomfortable and is counterproductive when questions are being asked to make the point that "I was right from the start!" or "Look how he blew that assignment." This does not mean that questions cannot be pointed or direct, but there needs to be an attitude of cooperation and progress that fosters relationships and moves the project toward a satisfactory conclusion. Just as in negotiation, framing a question properly makes a significant difference in its effectiveness.

Groups and projects generally only change and run more efficiently and effectively when someone asks a question. The simple "Why do we do this that way?" can lead to better processes and practices. The questions may be asked by a new employee or a seasoned veteran, but if the answers are unclear or don't make sense, it is an opportunity to improve.

Ask whatever questions you need to ask in order to understand your project or your contract. Ask questions of other people, but do not be afraid of asking questions of yourself. Going through a mental checklist can ensure that risks have been identified and opportunities explored. It can also boost your confidence level as you realize how well you understand the project or contract.

19.2 *Understanding answers*

After asking these questions, one has to decide what to do with the answers. Examined individually, the answers are simply points of data. Effective contract management requires moving those data points through a process so they become knowledge that moves the business forward.

Many articles have been written examining the terms *data*, *information* and *knowledge*. Most agree that the three move through a progression and require organization. Very simply, data is organized into information, and then information is put into context to become knowledge. This creative layering of data points into useful business information is in many ways the central theme of commercial management.

The initial data points may be very simple—for example, there is a contract for 500 components that your firm routinely orders. The price is $5000 CND inclusive of all taxes and shipping; the items are to be delivered on March 15 and payment will be made within 30 days of delivery. It seems like a regular order and raises no red flags. There are, however, some additional data points in the minds of the project staff that could make this anything but routine. First, someone in a different group—one that usually provides services to customers rather than manufacturing—requested the order. Second, the delivery date was just before the end of the first quarter. Placing this routine information together led to a conclusion that the transaction needed some questions answered beyond the order information. This was not a routine component order—it was to be included as part of a custom solution for a customer, which represented several million dollars of revenue that needed to be recognized by the end of the quarter. Failure to translate the information into business knowledge jeopardized the profitability of the company in its first quarter.

All of the information gained through previous experience contributes to the base of knowledge upon which new data can be interpreted and analyzed. While you may be managing a new project, the lessons learned from previous situations are invaluable. Recognizing warning signs that a deadline is slipping, people are not communicating, or a budget is running high comes largely from having seen and experienced it before. A key to professional development is learning from the experiences and mistakes of others.

19.3 *Documenting the results*

This book has been filled with case studies about the effects of documenting the understanding between the parties. Clearly recording the assumptions and expectations, and the rights and obligations is critical. Projects change. People change. Often the only thing left at the end of the day is the contract. If it appropriately reflects the original goals, and if it was kept current through an active change management process so that it reflects the current dealings, then it will help the business to achieve its objectives. If it was poorly constructed at the beginning and then relegated to a drawer, then even the minimal effort spent in its creation and maintenance was wasted.

Contracts are most effective when prepared with the business purpose in mind. That goes throughout the process, from documenting basic agreements to choosing clauses to managing change. Remembering the example of the snow shoveling in the introduction, we see that the contract must be suited to the purpose. That arrangement would never be adequate for a complex sale of product and services, but it worked quite nicely for removing snow from a sidewalk. Sometimes a simple purchase order is sufficient. Other transactions require more

sophisticated contracts. The demands of business today require us to choose the right contract to do the job effectively and efficiently.

19.4 Summary

Business is not slowing down. The world is not becoming simpler. Transactions are not becoming smaller. Change is not stopping. The headlines in the future will not likely reflect a rise in ethical behavior and a decrease of regulation. That is our reality—the challenge and the opportunity.

The processes described in this book are tools to guide individuals through the constantly changing business environment. Every project manager who takes simple steps to gain control and increase the chance for a successful project today leads to long-term corporate success in the future. But it begins with small, individual changes that are made today. In the end it is not simply anonymous corporations that act. As professionals we have a collective responsibility to make the contracts in our organization contribute to its success.

Appendix A: Countries that have ratified or accepted the CISG Convention

Albania
Argentina
Armenia
Australia
Austria
Belarus
Belgium
Bosnia and Herzegovina
Bulgaria
Burundi
Canada
Chile
China
Colombia
Croatia
Cuba
Cyprus
Czech Republic
Denmark
Dominican Republic
Ecuador
Egypt
El Salvador
Estonia
Finland
France
Gabon
Georgia

Germany
Greece
Guinea
Honduras
Hungary
Iceland
Iraq
Israel
Italy
Japan
Kyrgyzstan
Latvia
Lebanon
Lesotho
Liberia
Lithuania
Luxembourg
Mauritania
Mexico
Mongolia
Montenegro
Netherlands
New Zealand
Norway
Paraguay
Peru
Poland
Republic of Korea

Romania
Russian Federation
Serbia
Singapore
Slovakia
Slovenia
Spain
St Vincent and the Grenadines
Sweden
Switzerland

Syrian Arab Republic
The former Yugoslav Republic
    of Macedonia
Turkey
Uganda
Ukraine
United States of America
Uruguay
Uzbekistan
Zambia

Appendix B: Case studies

No 1: Key negotiation tactics

Peter Benjamin, the owner of an Australian chemical engineering consultancy, has been successful in China and is responsible for the design of many of the country's modern breweries. He was invited to submit a proposal for a huge Guangdong brewery.

Benjamin sent the Chinese a questionnaire, asking for information about specifications, resources, brewery capacity, products they planned to produce, budget, and business plans. The response he received convinced him to head to China to discuss a potential deal to build Guangdong province's largest brewery—a $20 million project. But, having heard from others about their China experiences, he decided to pitch only for the business in which his company had special technology to offer. "One of the first things you need to understand about China is that you can't compete against cheap, local rivals," he advises.

Preparing to negotiate

The Chinese party had no experience in designing breweries whereas, since 1983, Benjamin had built or redesigned all Australia's major breweries and most of its boutique breweries. Before starting negotiations, he did extensive research on the Chinese market, including its beer industry and the Guangzhou company. He found that, despite the company's listing on the Shanghai Stock Exchange, it had direct links to the Chinese government.

"If you're working with a brewery in China, you're working with the government, because the industry is so tightly regulated. I also found that the government department in charge of the alcohol industry is run by ex–Red Guards, so I knew I was dealing with people who had to report back to important government figures. I thought that, if I could find ways to make them look good in the eyes of their bosses, it would help in developing a beneficial business relationship," he said.

When Benjamin arrived in China, he discovered that the plans for the brewery were not as well defined as had initially appeared. "I decided my job was to be the expert, and I knew I should tell them what they needed, rather than let them tell me. It was clear they knew nothing about designing breweries." This would allow him to begin building relationships with the Chinese before the tendering process had begun. It would also give the Chinese lead negotiator face with his bosses (and the Chinese government officials), as he would be able to develop a better business brief using foreign technology. It also gave Benjamin's business a head start in the tender competition.

Shoring up advantage

Benjamin began to see the language barrier as an advantage. "Not knowing the language gave me carte blanche to completely change my mind on things I already had said, because I could use the excuse that I had not properly understood. They kept changing the negotiations on me, so it gave me the chance to do the same back and get away with it."

Benjamin had great respect for his competitors. They were professional managers, corporate people. But they also had superior attitudes toward the Chinese, and indeed also toward Benjamin and Australia. They refused to believe that a world-class brewery designer could be found in Australia.

After several weeks, the French and Belgian businesses pulled out, frustrated at the drawn-out negotiating process. In addition, no one on the French team liked Chinese cuisine, so returning home looked very attractive to them.

Benjamin, however, was a specialist chemical engineer who owned his own business, had already invested $350,000 in preparation, and was not inclined to walk away.

Patience pays

The Chinese team tried to use Benjamin's planned return date as leverage, in a bid to pressure him into agreeing to their price terms on the basis that he was leaving the country. But he recognized the ploy. "I realized they were dragging negotiations out until my departure, so I told them my date was flexible and I'd just stay until we finished. I acted as though I no longer had a deadline, and politely pointed out they were the ones who had to build a brewery within a certain time frame."

"There was one meeting in which one of the Chinese team became very angry and distressed. That night one of my interpreters told me that the individual had probably been testing my reaction. He explained that Chinese don't do business with people they don't know, and that sometimes they will use different emotions to see how the other party reacts under pressure.

But Benjamin believes it was more about relationships and face. "I put effort into helping them look good. I designed the brief with them using the latest technology. I helped solve other problems they had not considered, such as environment management that would save them money. I suggested my solutions would make their business a world leader. It was about giving them an opportunity to shine."

The last round of negotiations

The vice governor of Guangdong province finally stepped in, we understand, and made the decision in favor of Benjamin's company. Within forty-five minutes of his decision, the negotiation leader was on the phone to Benjamin at his hotel. "We want you to sign the contract," he said out of the blue and with no preamble. "Come to the office now. Also bring $2,000 to pay for the celebration banquet at lunchtime."

Benjamin and his team went directly to the provincial office. Before he signed the contract, he said to the team leader, "Thank you very much for your agreement to commission us to build your brewery. In consideration of that, we wish to present you with a five percent discount."

The step was artful. Bringing the project in five percent under budget gave face to everyone on the Chinese team, including the vice governor. They would not forget this.

This negotiation case study appears in Dr Bob March's excellent book 'The Chinese Negotiator' and is republished with his kind permission.

No 2: Commercial competence as a source of competitive advantage

Two of the world's largest corporations had done business together for more than 20 years. In fact, Company A was Company B's primary supplier of IT equipment and services, worth several hundred million dollars a year.

Company B's management became increasingly frustrated by the poor returns it felt were being achieved from its IT investments. Projects regularly ran over budget and behind schedule. When challenged, the IT function blamed Company A and claimed that there needed to be a change of architecture and supplier.

The resulting RFP was worth more than $1 billion and covered the supply of equipment to more than 100 countries. Company A was placed 4th in the technical evaluation and seemed to be out of the running, despite its proven ability to provide what Company B needed. Company A's Account Executive realized that internal politics were influencing Company B's evaluation. Some senior staff at Company B recognized that one of the major reasons for past failure was the inability of their own company as the customer to coordinate international projects. They understood that the key issue for any supplier would be its ability to compensate for Company B's lack of skills; they would need to have the commercial abilities and readiness to address the communication and coordination challenges of multi-national projects.

Company A's Account Executive called on a number of the top commercial experts internally—people from Finance, Contract Management and Legal who could shape the commercial offering and turn the company's global presence into a source of strength. He already had top executive support, but he knew that even this would not be enough for a customer made cynical by past promises that had not been met. It would be essential to explain not only what would be done to ensure success, but also how it would be achieved.

The negotiation revolved around demonstrating flexibility in contract terms and demonstration of their deep understanding of the process and resources needed for multi-country project implementation. Company A was the convincing winner in the commercial evaluation and—to the surprise of its competitors—won the bid.

No 3: It's not just the relationship that matters

Many people take the view that 'the contract' and 'the relationship' are quite distinct. Indeed, it is often said that good relationships do not need contracts. This attitude has in part been born of the fact that many traditional business relationships operated without contracts and often, when contracts are in place, they are referred to only when something goes wrong.

This attitude misses several key points, which were illustrated some years ago in a conversation with MITI, the Japanese Ministry of Industry.

Even after Japanese businesses started to become so successful as exporters in the 1980s, they made limited use of contracts. Commercial law was not well developed in Japan and many key relationships remained between Japanese companies, governed by the close connections of senior management. This collaborative, inter-dependent culture reduced the need for formal contracts.

However, increased exposure to international markets and the steady expansion of relationships with foreign firms—as both customers and suppliers—created growing awareness of the weaknesses in this approach. Misunderstandings became more frequent. Trading partners no longer felt the same pressures to conform. Claims, disputes and threats of litigation multiplied. Japanese management realized the need to develop a more structured approach to their trading relationships—to ensure greater formality in promises and commitments, to define processes through which these would be monitored and updated, and to provide protection in the event of disagreement.

This drove MITI to seek information on models and approaches for contract management, so that a traditional relationship-based culture could be supplemented by the discipline of good contract management. The growth of global markets has changed the purpose and value of contracts for most organizations, making the process and the document important tools that support good business relationships.

Appendix C: Glossary

Acceptance criteria: these are the criteria to determine that the business objectives have been met, and that the requirements have been delivered.

BAFO: Best And Final Offer

BATNA: 'best alternative to a negotiated agreement'

Battle of the forms: refers to the debate over whose form, contract, document, format, etc. that the contract will ultimately end up using. It comes from corporations pushing their form over the other sides, for various reasons.

Bid phase: the second phase in the contract management lifecycle. This phase explores the bidding and proposal activities undertaken by each party to determine the extent of the 'fit' between needs and capabilities. It examines the financial aspects of the proposed relationship and highlights the legal and regulatory issues surrounding bid and proposal activity.

Boilerplate: standard legal language (the small print) used by many companies, organizations or standard-setting bodies to simplify their contracting procedures. Boilerplate clauses are drawn from the long legal experience of large firms, and normally cannot be negotiated by the client or customer.

Change control process: a change control process defines how changes are to be managed throughout the project and contract lifecycles. It should identify the stages through which a requested change will pass. It should document: the change description; justification for the change; impact of the change; acceptance of the change; implementation of the change; verification of the change.

Civil law: a system of laws based on written legal code that govern disputes between individuals. Civil law is applied to issues involving property and contracts, as opposed to criminal acts.
[Source: The American Heritage® Dictionary of Business Terms Copyright © 2010 by Houghton Mifflin Harcourt Publishing Company.]

Commercial management: 'commercial' is often used to describe activities that are non-technical and can therefore embrace areas such as sales, marketing and business operations. Our definition embraces only those areas that are of direct relevance to the structuring, content and performance of the contract. We see the role of a 'commercial manager' or of the 'commercial process' to ensure that all relevant stakeholder views have been incorporated and evaluated, to ensure that the needs (of the customer) and capabilities (of the supplier) have been aligned. In this sense, we view the contract as a tool to undertake and oversee 'commercial assurance' of a deal or relationship and this may be from either a customer or supplier perspective.

Common law: common law is a body of legal rules that have been made by judges as they issue rulings on cases, as opposed to rules and laws made by the legislature or in official statutes.

Consortium: an alliance between companies by which, in tendering for a project, they make clear to the customer that it is their desire to work together, and that their tenders have been coordinated on that basis. A consortium has limited and entire scope, stands behind its own work and participants' work, has direct control of its own scope, and has less control over participants' scope.

Contract change: when the contract is negotiated and signed, the complete requirements of the final contract documentation represent the agreed position between the parties—the customer and the supplier. Once the contract document is signed, any alterations, enhancements, deletions or substitutions are, therefore, changes.

Contract close-out: the process that confirms the contract is officially terminated by performance and that there are no uncompleted legal obligations of either the customer or the supplier. Close-out assures that the correct payment is made to the supplier, the correct deliverables are received by the customer stakeholders, and administrative and fiscal obligations have been performed including disposition of property and assets.

Contract clause: a provision included in a written agreement or contract. A contract clause will address an aspect of the contract between parties, detailing the agreement to ensure all parties understand what is expected of the other.

Contract claim: a supplier can initiate a *contract claim* for a variety of reasons: the customer's failure to meet responsibilities, or having to do more work than agreed to, incurring more cost or having the program changed by the customer outside the formal change control process.

Contract management: the planning, monitoring and control of all aspects of the contract and the motivation of all those involved in it to achieve the contract objectives on time and to the specified cost, quality and performance.

Contract or Commercial Manager: the role assigned to contract management activities. These terms should be taken as indicating the performance of particular contract-related tasks, irrespective of who is actually performing them.

Contracting process: a high-performing business process through which successful contracts and trading relationships are formed and managed. Differences in the process will result from the types of contract or relationship that a business wishes to enable; for example, high volume commodities demand a fundamentally different model from complex services or major, long-term projects. The list of tasks remains consistent; the difference is over who performs those tasks, how they are performed, and the time it takes to reach completion.

Deliverable: a specific and defined obligation within the contract to deliver a particular item, which may be tangible (e.g. a manual, a product), or intangible (e.g. an idea or a service). 'The Deliverables' lie at the heart of most contracts.

Develop phase: the third phase in the contract management lifecycle. This phase is dedicated to the development of an appropriate form of contract and the considerations and issues that most frequently require attention. It provides a framework that should enable better understanding of the risks associated with the specific relationship that is being evaluated and also provides a base for negotiation planning.

Dispute: in contract management a dispute is an unresolved issue between contracting parties: the customer as the principal and the supplier as the provider of goods and services.

Dispute resolution: the method by which the parties to an agreement will reach resolution on disagreements. The dispute resolution process may involve a series of steps through which escalation of the dispute will occur. These may include internal forums (for example, executive management within each company) as well as external methods, such as Mediation, Arbitration or Litigation.

e-auctions: electronic auctions (or reverse electronic auctions as they are sometimes called) are on-line auctions where selected bidders submit offers electronically against the purchaser's specification.

ERP: enterprise resource planning

Final acceptance: applies when the contract is a project with milestones to be met. The last milestone may be final acceptance, or there may be a review and final acceptance after the last milestone is reached. It can occur at three distinct levels: unconditional acceptance, partial acceptance and total rejection.

Financial model: financial modeling usually refers to cash flow forecasting, which involves the creation of detailed models, which are used for strategic decision making.

Force majeure: can be translated as a 'superior force' or 'act of God'. When incorporated into a contract it usually provides that if a party does not perform an obligation under the contract (for example, provision of services) for reasons outside that party's control (such as a natural disaster or the outbreak of war), the other party will not make that party liable for non-performance.

Initiate phase: the first phase in the contract management lifecycle. This phase is devoted to ensuring understanding of markets and their interaction with business needs and goals. It explains the importance of aligning these factors with contract structures, terms, policies and practices, to increase the probability of successful trading relationships and the overall efficiency of the contracting process. Without such alignment, contracts rapidly become viewed as an impediment to doing business.

IPR: Intellectual Property Rights

Intellectual property (IP): includes inventions, patents, computer programs, product and service names, technical and business information, logos, artwork, geographic indication of source, industrial design, etc.

Joint venture: a cooperative business activity between two or more separate organizations for strategic purposes. These organizations can be privately owned companies, government agencies or other existing joint ventures. The joint venture may be implemented solely through contractual agreements to engage in cooperative or joint activities. In the marketing context, these are usually called 'Teaming Agreements' while in the development context they are more commonly termed 'Joint or Cooperative Development Agreements'. A true joint venture is implemented through a new entity in which a company and other parties make an equity (ownership right) investment.

KPI: key performance indicator

Lessons learned: a process for capturing and documenting key questions to continually ask throughout the life of the contract and the answers, such as "What went well?" and "How could that aspect have been managed better?" An effective process will allow people to find the information they require and to use the lessons of past experience.

Letter of Intent: is generally an agreement to agree. It outlines the terms between parties who have not formalized an agreement into a contract. Letters of Intent are generally not binding and unenforceable; they should be used with caution. Such letters indicate an intention to do something at a later date

Manage phase: the final phase in the contract management lifecycle. This phase examines the approaches needed to ensure successful implementation and management of the signed agreement. Many contracts span multiple years and it is frequently the case that they undergo major changes and, potentially, fundamental renegotiations. It is this phase that determines whether or not the results or outcomes envisaged at the time of contract signature are in fact achieved—or perhaps even exceeded.

Memorandum Of Understanding (MOU): a written document executed by certain parties which establishes intentions, policies or procedures of mutual concern. It does not require either party to obligate funds and does not create a legally binding commitment.

Negotiate phase: the fourth phase in the contract management lifecycle. This phase provides an in-depth guide to negotiation of a contract. It recognizes that a growing number of negotiations are today 'virtual', using technology as an alternative to face-to-face meetings. It also highlights many of the issues and challenges that contract negotiators tend to encounter, both within their own organization and with the behavior or attitudes of the other side.

NDA: non-disclosure agreement. A signed formal agreement in which one party agrees to give a second party confidential information about its business or products and the second party agrees not to share this information with anyone else for a specified period of time.

Outcome: the term used to describe the totality of what the contract is set up to deliver. For example, this could be an installed computer system with trained staff to use it, backed up by new working practices and documentation; a refurbished and equipped building with all the staff moved in and working; or the provision of repair and maintenance services that ensure high levels of product or service availability, compliance with safety regulations and on-going cost reductions.

Positional negotiation: the positional style tends to lead to what are termed win-lose results and correlates to a competitive negotiation strategy.

Prime contractor: has entire scope, stands behind its own work and subcontractors' work, has direct control of its own scope, and has contract control over subcontractors' scope.

Principled negotiation: the principled negotiation style leads to win-win results. It is employed when a negotiator is serious about finding a mutually acceptable solution and correlates to a collaborative negotiation strategy.

Procurement: the combined activities of acquiring services or goods, including ordering, arranging payment, obtaining transportation, inspection, storage, and disposal.

Procurement contracts: contracts of sale where an offer to buy or sell goods is made by acceptance of the offer and where the supplier transfers, or agrees to transfer, the property in goods to the buyer, for a money consideration called the price. The definition of the term 'goods' may vary according to the law enacted for the territory.

Request for Information: RFI: the customer has little information about the solution and needs to explore an idea or get information from suppliers about how they would solve the customer's needs.

Request for Proposal: RFP: used to solicit proposals from suppliers where the customer has strong and well thought out business requirements.

Request for Quotation: RFQ: the customer has precise information about purchase (usually a commodity item), there is little variation in the product and the customer is primarily interested in the best price on the best terms.

ROI: Return on investment

RFx: [a combination of] any of the following—RFI, RFQ, RFP

Service Level Agreement (SLA) is a comprehensive tool [document] to monitor and manage supplier performance for the provision or receipt of the services provided. The SLA typically identifies the fixed measurements for the delivery of the services and spells out measurements for performance and consequences for failure. It must include:

- Levels of required performance
- Consequences for failure to reach or maintain these levels
- Descriptions of the parties' roles and responsibilities in achieving the performance levels

Statement of Work (SOW): is a document describing the essential and technical requirements for items, materials, or services, including the standards that will be used to determine whether the requirements have been met. A Statement of Work may be simple or complex, flexible or definitive, depending on what it describes

A **subcontractor** has limited scope, stands behind its own work, and has direct control of its own scope.

Termination: ending the contractual relationship before its natural, or originally anticipated, end date. Termination may be for convenience, where the parties agree to part ways or end the contract mutually; or for cause, where there is a breach of the agreement.

Terms and conditions: a *term* is a part of the contract that addresses a specific subject. Contract clauses contain terms. A *condition* is a phrase that either activates or suspends a term. A condition that activates a term is called a condition precedent. A condition that suspends a term is called a condition subsequent.

A *condition* is a phrase that either activates or suspends a term. A condition that activates a term is called a condition precedent. A condition that suspends a term is called a condition subsequent.

TCO: total cost of ownership. TCO calculations can include the obvious: purchase cost, implementation costs, maintenance and support costs. Thorough cost of ownership analysis embodies a cradle-to-grave view of costs: from resources required to develop the business case, draft the Request For Proposals (RFP) and manage the bid process, through to decommissioning and disposal of the asset.

Turnkey project/contract: the term 'turnkey' in business terminology means that the buyer needs only to turn the 'key' to the system [or facility] and it will work. Integral parts of a contract to buy a turnkey system [or facility] of any type are the terms and conditions for the acceptance of the system [or facility] and when/how payments will be made. The contract must define what it means for the system [or facility] to work, and what is expected of the system [or facility], so that the buyer can accept the system [or facility] and the supplier can be paid/recognize revenue.

UNCISG: UN Convention on Contracts for the International Sale of Goods. Applies when trading internationally—the CISG applies to seventy-five nations, including most of the major trading nations. Note that the UK has not signed up to the CISG at the time of writing.

UCC: Uniform Commercial Code. Applies when trading within the US

WTO: World Trade Organization

Index